THE GRATITUDE PRESCRIPTION FOR KIDS

Navigating Illness with Thankfulness and Positivity

Discover How Gratefulness and Practicing Optimism Can Help Kids Feel Better Faster During Sickness or Injuries

© Copyright 2024

All rights reserved. No part of this book may be reproduced, stored, or transmitted in any form by any means, electronic or mechanical, including photocopying, recording, or any information storage and retrieval system, without prior written permission from the publisher, except for personal use by the purchaser.

Disclaimer: This book is intended to help children and their families explore gratitude and the idea that focusing on positive thoughts and feelings can attract well-being and healing during times of illness or recovery. While the information presented is based on personal experience, research, and practical techniques, it is not intended to replace professional medical advice or treatment. Always seek guidance from a licensed healthcare or mental health professional before applying any of the suggestions or activities provided.

The author and publisher make no guarantees about the effectiveness of the practices shared and are not responsible for any outcomes, errors, or omissions. By reading and applying the content of this book, the reader agrees that any use of the material is at their own discretion and risk. The information provided should be used as a supportive tool alongside professional care.

Table of Contents

Introduction 1
   Dear Parents/Caregiver 2
   Dear Kids 5

Part 1: Understanding Illness and How Our Minds Work 7
   Chapter 1: What Is Illness? 7
      What Happens to Your BODY When You are Sick 8
      What Happens to Your MIND When You are Sick 9
   Chapter 2: How Illness Affects the Way You Think and Feel 16
      Mind-Body Connection 16
      Positive Thoughts = Positive Energy 17

Part 2: Gratitude for Healing 19
   Chapter 3: Gratitude: The Magic Power of Thankfulness 19
      Why is Gratitude a Healing Superpower? 19
   Chapter 4: Your Body is Listening... and Healing 29
   Chapter 5: The Power of Small Things 33
      Small Moments, Big Magic 33
      Grateful Thoughts HIGHLIGHT More Reasons to Be Grateful 35
      Gratitude Creates a Positive Cycle 37
   Chapter 6: Thankfulness for Support 41
   Chapter 7: Finding Gratitude When Sick 47
      Ways to Discover Gratitude 47
      Self-Compassion: It Is Okay to Feel Down Sometimes 49
   Chapter 8: From Bad Days to Better Days 52
      Accepting and Releasing Unhelpful Thoughts and Feelings 52
      Changing Negative Thoughts and Feelings to Positive Ones 55

Part 3: The Law of Attraction for Healing 58
   Chapter 9: The Law of Attraction - The Magic Power of Focus and Intention. 58
      How Does the Law of Attraction Work? 60
   Chapter 10: Attracting Physical Healing 65
      Pay Attention to Small Signs of Improvement 66

Release Your Fears.. 67

Chapter 11: Attracting Emotional Strength... 70

Chapter 12: Affirmations: Positive Statements for Healing 75

Chapter 13: Vision Boards: Seeing Your Future Healthy Self 80

Chapter 14: Believing and Staying Positive During Tough Days........ 85

Part 4: Gratitude in Action for Healing.. 90

Chapter 15: Gratitude in Nature 90

Chapter 16: Creative Gratitude 97

    Why Creative Gratitude Matters 97

    Gratitude Through Art.. 99

    Gratitude Through Crafts... 99

    Gratitude Through Photography 100

    Gratitude Through Baking or Cooking 100

    Gratitude Through Writing 100

    Gratitude Through Music... 101

Chapter 17: Starting a Gratitude Journal...................................... 104

    How Can Writing About Gratitude Attract More Reasons to Be Thankful? 104

    Top 10 Tips to Starting a Gratitude Journal 105

    Advice for Common Journaling Problems 110

Part 5: Living a Life Full of Gratitude and Positive Intentions.........112

Chapter 18: Staying Grateful Every Day 112

Chapter 19: Attracting Good Things Every Day 115

Chapter 20: The Light at the End of the Tunnel............................. 121

    Looking After Yourself 121

    Dealing with Setbacks 127

Chapter 21: Sharing Your Story... 131

Chapter 22: Gratitude and Positivity Beyond Injury and Illness 133

Conclusion 137

Bonus: My "Wishes Come True" Box 138

A Message from Emma 141

References 143

Introduction

Hi there! I know being sick or injured is really tough. It is just no fun at all, is it? But you know what? Even during tough times, there are some powerful and amazing things you can do to feel better inside and out. I actually like to think of them as "**healing superpowers!**"

First up is something called **gratitude**. It is about being thankful for good things—no matter how small they may seem. The cool part? Gratitude not only helps you feel better, it also has this amazing ability to make difficult things seem small—tiny even!

Then, there is the superpower of **positivity**. It is about choosing to feel, think, and be optimistic. Why? Well, think of positivity like a big, cool magnet. If you are positive, then you *attract* other positive stuff to come your way.

Here is a simple example: If you smile at someone, they often smile back, right? Well, there you go; that is positivity in action! You did something kind and positive, and it inspired someone to do the same. ☺

Now, imagine spending a lot of time beaming positivity. It is pretty cool to think how much positive stuff you get back, right?

So, in this book, you are going to learn all about using these two amazing superpowers—gratitude and positivity—and you will understand how they can help you with your healing.

You will explore cool ideas and do lots of fun activities to help you stay strong, positive, and thankful even though you are going through something tough right now.

And you know what? My guess is that by the time you are finished with this book, you will feel so much better!

Nurse Valentina

Valentina Fox, RN

Gratitude and Positive Mindset Advocate

But first, something real quick for parents or caregivers...

Dear Parents/Caregiver

Do you remember where you were and what you were doing on December 26, 2004? You are probably thinking something about Christmas and how it is such a wonderful time for the entire family. Me? I remember staring at the TV screen.

The news just came on about the massive tsunami that hit Thailand, and it was heart wrenching and devastating to watch. Little did I know that I would be facing a "personal tsunami" just a few hours later.

You see, my 18-month-old daughter, Emma, had been battling the flu for WEEKS. We saw a doctor immediately, of course, and she was prescribed antibiotics, but they did not seem to help. Oh, she enjoyed the festivities, the vibrant colors and smells, and the gifts as any toddler would—but my mommy heart ached to see her so sick.

So, on December 26, 2004, we let Emma sleep in as my husband and I stayed glued to the news about the tsunami when suddenly, **I heard Emma scream, "Mommy!!!"**

I did not even pause to think or look at my husband. I jumped out of the sofa and ran to my daughter. The way she shouted... **I just knew something was wrong.**

I ran to Emma's room and saw my daughter extremely pale, but when I touched her forehead, she was burning up. I checked her temperature, and it was registered at 40°C. My husband and I quickly got her into the car, and **within minutes, we were at the hospital emergency room**.

I guess the first clue I had at just how serious things were was when the doctor immediately ordered a blood test. Within a few hours, the doctor came out and told us that Emma **had Acute Lymphoblastic Leukemia (ALL)**.

I was dumbfounded and totally robbed of speech. I was in a haze and barely realized that our doctor was scheduling Emma the following day for a Port-a-Cath (a small medical device implanted under the skin for easy access to veins during chemotherapy).

We all have our methods of coping with shock and pain. Some might go into denial, and others might express extreme anger at the unfairness of it all. Me? I turned my internal positivity switch to "On" and sprung to action. All I thought of was, "What do we need to do to make her better?" And I did not mean just "feel better," I wanted her to beat this!

From that day on, I blocked everything that did not contribute to my daughters' health and wellness. I embraced every good day, every positive thought, every optimistic idea, and every ounce of hope. I poured this all on my daughter, and I encouraged her young mind to do the same.

- After every round of chemotherapy... *be grateful, my darling daughter, for each day you can do this.*
- During sleepless nights... *chin up, my love; tomorrow is another day, and it will be amazing.*
- Whenever she felt tired and down... *focus, dearest, on the strength you have gained and the love surrounding you.*

Did it work? With a grateful heart, I am happy to share that Emma is now 21 years old and has just graduated with a degree in Business, majoring in Accounting and Finance. (You can read her message to you on page 141.)

So yes, I believe with all my heart that **gratitude and positivity** not only helped us get through the next two years of her battle with ALL, but they also played a crucial role in her healing! To me, they are **emotional and mental medicine**.

Why This Book Is Also for You
In the following pages, your child will be presented with a complete gratitude and positivity toolbox. They will explore ideas and activities to strengthen their mindset and, hopefully, their bodies too. And that "healing?" It is for you, too!

I know how hard it is, mentally and emotionally, to care for a sick child. And each day that they are happy and strong is a GREAT DAY for you as well. So, I recommend that you go through these pages, too.

Share this journey with them. You will not only support their healing but also nurture your own. Trust me; it will build a path of resilience and hope for both of you.

Dear Kids

Hi again! 👋 Are you ready for your gratitude and positivity journey?

You know, I made this book especially for you. So why don't you really put your stamp on it by doing the **About Me** activity on the next page? You can use colors, pens, pencils, crayons, and stickers. You can also paste your picture or draw stuff—whatever suits you.

Oh, and here is a gentle reminder: It is 100% okay to take your time with this book. There is no need to rush, and there is definitely no right or wrong answer. Just do your best and have fun. This book is YOUR book, and it is a safe space where you can share your thoughts and feelings.

So, whether you are doing an activity, practicing gratitude, or thinking positive thoughts—go at your own pace. Remember that every step, big or small, helps you feel stronger inside and out!

ALL ABOUT ME!

ME

My name is _____

I am _____ years old.

I live in _____

I am excited about _____
_____
_____

MY FAVORITE ACTIVITIES

MY FAVORITE FOODS

WHAT I LIKE ABOUT MYSELF...

My goals for this year are:

1. _____
2. _____
3. _____

Part 1:
Understanding Illness and How Our Minds Work

CHAPTER 1:
WHAT IS ILLNESS?

Everyone gets sick, but not everybody gets sick the same way. It is interesting how two people can do the same things or be exposed to the same things, but one might get ill while the other one stays perfectly fine. Other times, two people can have the same illness but show different symptoms and feel differently. Hmmm...

Illness is when your body is not working the way it should, and it could mean a lot of things. It could mean that you have caught something like a cold or the flu, and this might make you sneeze, cough, or run a fever.

Other times, it can be something more serious, like when a part of your body is not working right for a long time. For example, when someone has asthma, their lungs do not always work properly, making it hard to breathe. Or, like when my daughter was sick, her blood was not working like it should, making her feel very tired and weak most of the time.

Now, your body is ALWAYS trying to keep you healthy by fighting off germs like bacteria and viruses. But sometimes, these unhealthy things are a bit too strong, and you end up feeling sick. During times like these, your body may need extra help to get better. That is why doctors give you medicine and why resting, eating healthy food, and having the right mindset are so important!

By the way, being ill is not the same as having an injury. An injury is when a part of your body gets hurt—like if you twist and sprain your ankle, get a cut, or break a bone. So, you can say that having an illness is being sick "inside the body" while having an injury is being sick "outside the body."

When you are injured, though, your body still needs time and TLC (tender loving care) to bounce back. Your body may swell, hurt, need stitches, or need protection like a bandage or cast.

Still, just like when you are ill, your body is working really hard to fix the injury and get you back to feeling strong again. And just like when you are feeling under the weather, the way you THINK can really speed up your recovery!

What Happens to Your BODY When You are Sick

Your body is like a 24-hour superhero! It is constantly fighting off germs—tiny invaders like bacteria or viruses—that can make you feel unwell. So, you can imagine that when you do fall ill, your body is like going to battle to protect you. It is putting in a ton of effort to beat and shoo away whatever is making you ill.

So, really, when you have a runny nose, a cough, or a fever, these are signs that your body is working hard to fight the germs.

For example, a fever means your body is cranking up the heat to help destroy the germs inside. If you have a cough or a runny nose, it is your body doing its thing to clear out the bad stuff from your lungs and nose. Cool, huh?

What Happens to Your MIND When You are Sick

When you are sick, your body is not the only thing that is working hard—your mind is too! Your mind is like a "remote control" that influences your thoughts and feelings, and when you are not feeling well, it can definitely throw you off a bit.

Sometimes, when you are not feeling well, you might feel sad, worried, or even frustrated. That is totally normal! Your mind might be thinking about how much you want to feel better, how hard it is to do certain things because you are tired, or how you might be missing out on a lot of fun activities with your friends.

But here is the good news: Just like your body has a defense team fighting germs, your mind can be strong and a "fighter," too!

Imagine your mind like a Coach. It cheers your body on as it fights your illness or injury. Now, if a coach is feeling down or negative, it is harder for the team to win, right?

But when a coach is positive and encouraging, WOWZA! The whole team gets stronger and can accomplish many amazing things!

So, what can you do to turn your mind into an awesome Coach? You guessed it—by focusing on good things and being grateful for them, and by thinking positive thoughts (to attract more positive stuff).

If you can do this, even when you do not feel your best, then "Coach Mind" can cheer, inspire, and stimulate "Human Body" to stay strong and get better faster.

In the next chapters, we are going to dive into some awesome activities that will help you **train your mind to become a fantastic healing coach for your body**. But before we dive in, take a moment to check out the quick activity on the next page.

Activity #1: Mind and Body Check-In

When you are sick, it is common to zero in on where you are hurting and all the discomfort you are feeling. So much so that we often forget to notice all the other body parts that are doing just fine! For example, when you are feeling sick to your stomach, it is easy to think only about being nauseous and the pain and forget that your arms, legs, and heart are still strong and amazing.

So, this exercise has two goals. It is about acknowledging where you hurt AND realizing where you DON'T hurt. Why?

First, it is important to be aware of things. Ignoring or pretending your pain or illness is not there won't make it go away. In fact, it can sometimes make things worse because you cannot fix what you refuse to accept. (Pretty deep, huh?)

Second, realizing where you DON'T hurt reminds you that your body is still amazing and working hard to keep you strong, even when some parts of it are unwell.

So, this exercise is all about finding balance in how you see things. It is about "keeping it real" but also recognizing and valuing the awesome things your body can still do. Okay, let's go!

Hey, make sure to grab a pen and some paper, or even a notebook or journal, so you can jot down notes while you work through this exercise.

Step 1. Quick Body Check-In

Take a minute to scan your body, starting from the top of your head and then slowly working your way down right to your toes.

Are you feeling any aches or pains right now? If so, write down WHERE you are experiencing the pain. For example, suppose you have a headache. Where exactly are you feeling it? On your forehead? At the top of your head? At the back of your neck?

Step 2. Describe What You are Feeling

This section focuses on really paying attention to what your physical pain feels like, helping you get a clearer picture of it. For example, you might want to use words like *sharp*, *aching*, *stiff*, or *numb* to really capture what you are feeling.

For example, if your shoulders are feeling heavy, you might say, "My shoulders feel stiff and tense."

What is the point of all this?

You know when you are talking to a friend, and you notice that they are not in the mood? You ask what is up, and they might say, "I am really angry right now?" And then you follow up with, "What do you mean?" And then they reply, "I am just so mad!"

That conversation right there was not very helpful, was it? (You STILL do not know what is going on!)

When you are ill, the more accurate you are at explaining WHAT and WHERE you are feeling sick, the better. First, it can make it easier for your doctor and other adults to support you. But this is also important for YOU.

The better you understand yourself, the better you will understand how your body is dealing with your illness and what could help you feel better. It is like getting to know your body's signals more clearly.

When you can accurately describe your pain—whether it is *sharp*, *dull*, *throbbing*, or *tight*—you will feel more in control and aware of what is going on. Hey, you are not just sitting back and letting your pain take over; you are paying attention to it so you can deal with it better. (Yep, you are the boss!)

Step 3. Emotional Check-In
Next, take a sec to see how you are doing emotionally or mentally. How are you really feeling? Are you feeling anxious, stressed, or maybe overwhelmed? If so, where do you feel that mental and emotional tension hanging out in your body? Oh yes, thoughts and emotions can be felt or experienced in your body!

For example, when you are nervous about an exam or a big event, you might feel butterflies in your stomach or feel your heart racing. If you are feeling sad, you might notice a heavy feeling in your chest or sense your body feeling more sluggish. Even happiness can be felt physically. When you smile, it can make you feel all light and happy inside, like a cozy warmth spreading through you.

So, let's do this again? How are you feeling? Write it out below.

I feel _____.

I am feeling this on my _____.

Step 4. Shift Focus

Now for the good stuff: Take a step back and consider what **doesn't** hurt or where you feel good. Often, when we focus on pain or discomfort, we totally overlook the parts of ourselves that are doing just fine.

For example, are your legs strong? Is your head still in the game, even with that headache? Can you still make things with your hands, see the world with your eyes, and feel love in your heart?

Take a minute to write down at least **three** things that feel strong, useful, or just plain awesome about your body or life right now.

Examples:
I have got some seriously strong legs! I can still walk, you know.
I am really glad I have no headaches today and can think clearly today. It is a good day!
I love my dog, Charlie!

Hey, do not overthink this. Just write down whatever comes to mind. Remember, there is no right or wrong answer here!

Good stuff 1: _____

_____

Good stuff 2: _____

_____

Good stuff 3: _____

_____

Step 5. Optional: Share with Someone You Trust

If you feel like it, talk about this exercise with someone close to you. Talking about what you are going through—both the tough stuff and the good stuff—can help you feel better.

CHAPTER 2:
HOW ILLNESS AFFECTS THE WAY YOU THINK AND FEEL

As we briefly discussed in the previous chapter, when you are ill or injured, it doesn't just affect your body—it sort of messes with your mind and emotions, too. This is because your body and mind are totally linked, and they are constantly chatting with each other. Think of it like a conversation where what one says influences the other.

That is, what is going on in your body can totally affect the way you think and feel... and, on the flip side, what you think and feel can totally change the way your body works! This cool concept is called the **mind-body connection**.

Mind-Body Connection

Just so you know, the **mind-body connection** is not just an idea. This is totally legit and based on science.

For example, when you are feeling happy or excited, your body releases chemicals like *endorphins* and *dopamine*, which make you feel good and energized.

On the other hand, when you are stressed or sad, your body reacts by releasing chemicals like *cortisol*. This can make you feel tired and tense or even cause physical pain like headaches or stomach aches.

This mind-body connection thing is important to know because it means that **your thoughts and emotions have real energy**—they can influence how good or bad your body feels.

For example, when you are sick, you might notice that your mood is not exactly on the "happy" and "excited" spectrum. In fact, you may feel downright sad, gloomy, frustrated, or even angry. This happens because when your body is trying to heal, it uses A LOT of energy, which can leave you feeling wiped out, both physically and emotionally.

Now, this *physical state* can make you *think* stuff like, "I cannot do anything," or "I will never get better!" Sadly, these negative thoughts can really bring you down even more, making you feel sad or hopeless, and that can make your body tense up and become more stressed. And when your body is stressed, it focuses more on managing that stress than on healing, which can really slow down how quickly you can recover.

This is where the energy of your thoughts comes in.

Positive Thoughts = Positive Energy

Think of your body as a living and breathing battery that powers everything you do.

Negative energy: When you think negative thoughts—like "I will never get better!"—it totally drains the battery faster. It makes your body tense up, making it harder for your immune system to work at its best.

Positive energy: On the flip side, positive thoughts like "I am doing my best to heal" and emotions like gratitude, hope, or calmness—are like recharging your battery. They help your body relax so it can focus more on fighting off illness and heal itself.

Negative vibes zap your energy.
Positive vibes recharge your mental and physical battery!

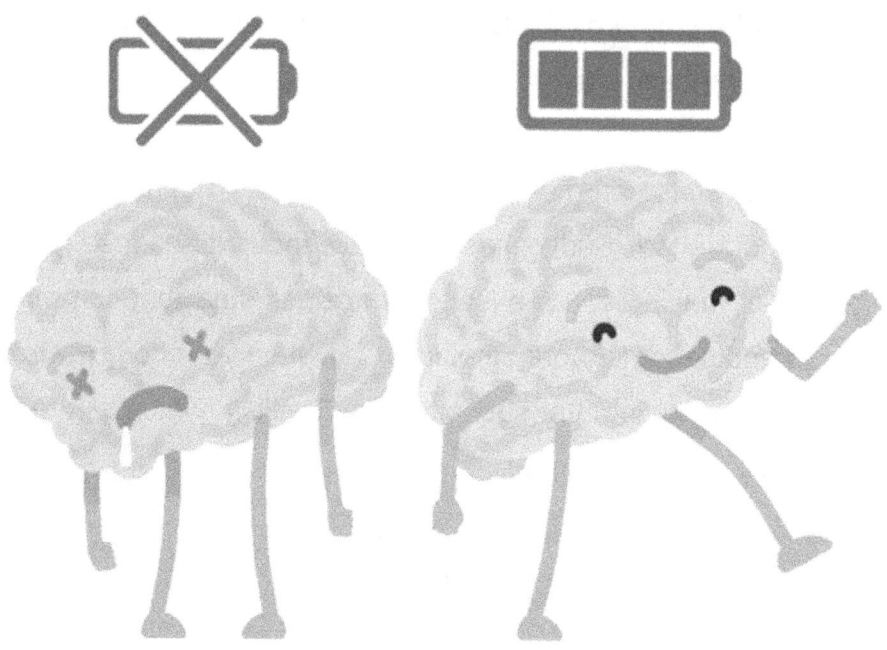

So, if you are feeling a bit down or negative, the best thing you can do to help yourself heal is to *change* the way you think and feel. Doing this will send powerful, positive signals (energy) to your body, helping it heal better and faster.

Luckily, there are PLENTY of cool things you can do to start transforming that negative energy into positive energy for your body! Everything you need to know is outlined for you in the next chapters.

For now, one of the most important things to remember is that your mind is incredibly powerful! Even though you cannot control everything that happens in your body, you can definitely control how you respond to it. Oh yes, "Coach Mind" can really change the game!

Part 2: Gratitude for Healing

CHAPTER 3:
GRATITUDE: THE MAGIC POWER OF THANKFULNESS

Gratitude is all about being thankful for the good things you have got going. It is focusing on what you have instead of what you are missing. And on what is going right rather than what is going wrong.

Gratitude doesn't mean pretending you are not sick or ignoring that fact. It is noticing the other stuff that is going well, even though you are injured or not feeling your best. For example:

- You have a nasty cold... *but your body is working hard to help you heal.*
- You are missing out on all the activities at school... *but you are giving your body the time it needs to get better.*
- You cannot go outdoors... *but you have a cozy space inside your home where you can rest and relax.*
- You miss hanging out with your friends...*but you can still be in touch with them through a phone call or video chat.*

Why is Gratitude a Healing Superpower?
Gratitude is not just something that makes you feel good—it actually has a REAL impact on your brain and body. Let's look at how gratitude works... based on cool science!

- **Gratitude Boosts Happiness**
Gratitude triggers the release of chemicals in your brain, like **dopamine** and **serotonin**, which are known as "feel-good" chemicals.

Dopamine is linked to feelings of "pleasure" or "reward," while serotonin helps regulate mood. When you practice gratitude, you are recognizing something good in your life, right? The brain releases dopamine because you are feeling a sense of pleasure or happiness. (Hey, if you think about something you are grateful for, you are bound to be happy!) Next, your body releases serotonin to help maintain that positive mood.

And here is something really cool—research has shown that people who practice gratitude regularly tend to be more optimistic and happier about their lives.[1]

- **Gratitude Reduces Stress**
When you are stressed, your body releases a hormone called **cortisol**, which can make you feel tense and anxious. Now, too much cortisol floating around can actually mess with your body's ability to heal from illness.

But here is the good news—research shows that practicing gratitude can lower cortisol levels by up to 23%![2] So, low cortisol = less stress = your body has more energy to focus on healing and fighting off illness.

- **Gratitude Rewires Your Brain**
When you are sick, it is natural to think about the pain or discomfort you are experiencing. But if you can switch gears and think about what is going well and be grateful for it, you actually change how your brain

works.[3] Scientists call this cool thing **neuroplasticity**, which means your brain can form new connections based on what you are thinking.

So, what is the deal with this? It means that by focusing on gratitude, you are training your brain to notice the positive stuff more often. This makes it easier to feel good, even during tough times.

- **Gratitude Helps Improve Physical Health**

  Here is where gratitude really shows its superpower: Studies have found that people who regularly practice gratitude tend to be healthier than those who do not.[4]

When you practice gratitude regularly, it can really make a difference. People have found that it helps them feel less pain, boosts their immune systems, and even speeds up recovery when they are sick.

Just WOW, right?!

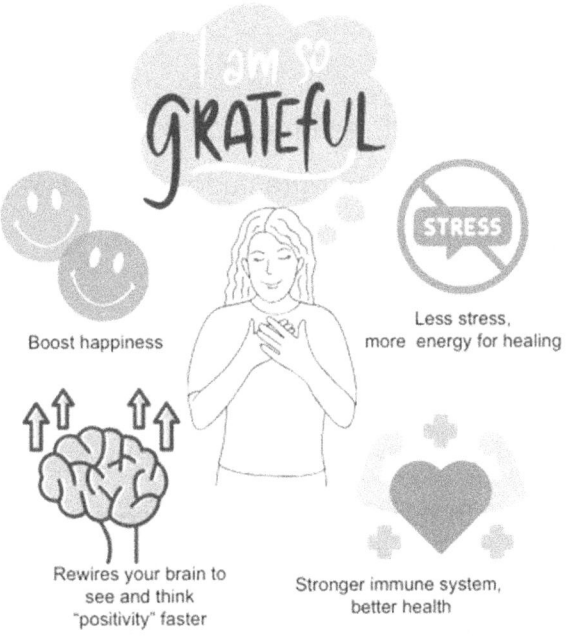

But you know what is really awesome about gratitude? The thing, person, or situation that you can be thankful for ALREADY EXISTS! You do not have to wait or hope for something to be thankful for. It is already there; all you have to do is take a moment to notice it.

Go ahead, close your eyes right now, and take a few deep breaths. What are you thankful for at this exact moment?

Seriously, do not overthink this. You could just be grateful for the air you breathe, the clothes you have on, or even the comfortable chair you are sitting in. You might be thankful for a warm meal or simply the fact that you have a moment of peace. Whatever pops into your head, no matter how small, it is worth appreciating! The goal is to focus on what is going well *right now,* even if it is something super simple.

Hold on, there is more to it! Gratitude is not just about what you think. If you really want to tap into some amazing healing powers, you should definitely throw "appreciation" into the mix.

Think of this this way: Gratitude is something you FEEL inside; appreciation is something you DO to express your gratitude. (This statement is so powerful; seriously, even adults often miss it!)

For example:
Gratitude: I am grateful for the milk and cookies I enjoyed for my afternoon snack.
Appreciate: Hey, Mom, thanks for the milk and cookies you gave me earlier.

Gratitude: I am grateful for the *Get Well Soon* card my bestie sent.

Appreciate: Send a quick SMS... Hi [friend], thanks again for the card. That was really thoughtful.

Gratitude: I am really thankful that I can chill in my room and binge whatever I want on Netflix.

Appreciate: Mom/Dad, thanks for giving me some space to relax and watch my favorite shows in my room. I really needed that alone time.

Activity #2: Count Your Blessings, Not Your Burdens

We take sooooo many things for granted that we usually miss all the good stuff. Now, it is not like we do it on purpose. We just kinda forget to REALLY LOOK at what is going well.

Take me for example: Every day, I walk by my front yard on my way to my car. The other day, I tripped over something and hurt my toe against a stone. I was huffing and puffing, and all of a sudden, I was annoyed at my "ugly" yard.

When I got into my car, I came to my senses (ha! ha!) and realized that EVERY SINGLE DAY, I walk by my front yard with no issues. So, before I drove away, I looked at my yard and said, "Thank you for being such a colorful and sturdy yard!" I felt so good, and I swear my toe barely hurt anymore.

So this exercise is for you to take some time and think—REALLY THINK—about what you are grateful for, okay? You just might be surprised to realize just how great you have got it.

Step 1. Grab Pen and Paper
Start by getting a notebook, journal, or a piece of paper, along with a pen or pencil. Next, write the date at the top of a page to help you keep track of your progress as you start practicing gratitude.

Step 2. List 3 PEOPLE You are Grateful For
Think about **three people** who have been kind or helpful to you. You do not need to rank them or anything like that. Just take a deep breath and write down the first three people that pop into your head and why you are grateful for them.

Example:

I am grateful for my Dad for coming home early from work today to bring me to my doctor's appointment.

I am grateful for: _____
_____

I am grateful for: _____
_____

I am grateful for: _____
_____

Step 3. List 3 EVENTS OR EXPERIENCES You are Grateful For

Now, think about **three events or experiences** that made you feel good, even if they were small moments.

Example:

I am grateful for the time my teacher praised me for doing well on my project.

I am grateful for: _____
_____

I am grateful for: _____
_____

I am grateful for: _____
_____

Step 4. List 3 THINGS You are Grateful For

Next, list **three things** you enjoy or appreciate in your life. These could be physical objects, simple comforts, etc.

Example:
I am grateful for my favorite book because it helps me escape into another world.

I am grateful for: _____
_____

I am grateful for: _____
_____

I am grateful for: _____
_____

Step 5. Check Out Your List!

Once you have completed your list, take a few moments to go through it and really feel the gratitude for each person, event, and thing you wrote down. Feel that gratitude! Truly, recognizing the positive aspects of your life can help shift your focus away from any negative thoughts or burdens.

Food for thought: Did you like doing this activity? If you did, consider doing it regularly like every week or at the start of every month!

Activity #3: Stop-Embrace-Express (a.k.a. SEE)

In the previous activity, you listed people, events, and things for which you are grateful. Now, we are going to *extend* that gratefulness and dive into appreciation.

Step 1. Stop and take a moment to pause.
Go back to the list you did in the previous exercise, take a moment, and select a person, event, or thing for which you want to express thankfulness.

Example:
I choose my Dad.
I choose _____

Step 2. Embrace the feeling of gratitude.
Once you have made your choice, fully focus on it. Embrace the feelings that gratitude brings, and let all the good vibes wash over you. Imagine this moment like a warm light growing inside you—notice how awesome it feels to focus on something positive.

Step 3. Express your gratitude!
Now that you are feeling all those good vibes, it is time to spread the love! The best move is to connect with the person you are thankful for or anyone who played a part in making that awesome event or thing happen.

Examples:
Hi, Dad! I know you are busy at work, so I just wanted to say thanks for coming home early to bring me to my doctor's appointment.

Hi, Jerome! Guess what? I just remembered our school camping trip last month, and I want to thank you for letting me borrow your flashlight when mine died! Hahaha

Do you want to practice expressing your gratitude? Write it out here:

_____

_____

_____

_____

_____

If you are not comfortable connecting with the person just yet, that is totally fine. You can still express your thankfulness by getting all creative, like drawing a picture that represents the moment.

It is all about showing your appreciation in a way that feels genuine to you!

CHAPTER 4:
YOUR BODY IS LISTENING... AND HEALING

All right, so in Chapter 2, we covered the whole mind-body connection thing. Do you remember what it is?

Your mind and body are like best friends—they are completely connected and can totally influence each other. When you are not feeling great physically, it can totally mess with your mood, leaving you feeling sad, frustrated, or even angry. And the worse your mood dips, the tougher it becomes for your body to concentrate on healing. It is kind of like being stuck in a cycle that just keeps dragging you down.

But here is the cool part—if you work on shifting your mood (like moving from feeling sad and frustrated to feeling happy and hopeful), you can speed your body's healing process. Think of it as sending your body a positive message: "Hey, we've got this!"

Then, in Chapter 3, we talked about how science PROVES the mind-body connection, such as how gratitude can make your brain release "feel good" chemicals and how it can lower your stress levels, which is super important. When your body is not busy dealing with stress, it can really put its energy into healing itself.

So, what does this all mean? It means that **your body is ALWAYS listening to your thoughts**! And when you mentally send it love and gratitude, you give it the encouragement it needs to heal faster.

For example, if you are recovering from a cold or an injury, try closing your eyes, taking a deep breath, and saying something like, "Thank you, body, for fighting this illness," or "Thanks, body, for getting stronger every day." It might seem simple, but these small gestures of gratitude make a BIG difference in helping your body focus on getting well.

Activity #4: Love and Gratitude Notes to Your Body

This activity is a cool way to show some love and appreciation for your body, which can really help with healing. It shows you how to recognize and value all the incredible things your body can do, especially during those times when you are not feeling great and trying to recover.

Step 1. Find a Quiet Space

Look for a chill spot where you can really zone in and not get distracted. Take a deep breath in... and let it out. Do it at least one more time. Now, think about your body and start exploring how hard it is working to keep you healthy.

Step 2. Scan Your Body

Close your eyes and do a quick check-in with your body. Start with your head. How does it feel? Next, shift your focus to your neck, shoulders, arms, and hands. Keep going through each part of your body. Notice if any part feels sore, tense, or tired. Do not get stuck on anything. For example, if your shoulders feel sore, just acknowledge that (i.e., my shoulders feel sore) and move on. Do not get stuck on it.

Step 3. Write or Draw Your Gratitude Notes

Now, gently open your eyes and grab a pen and some paper, or if you prefer, a notebook or journal. Alright, take a moment to focus on your body again. This time, as you think about each part, try writing or drawing a little note of thanks for what it does for you.

It is important to appreciate the parts of you that feel great, and even the ones that are struggling, because they are ALL putting in the effort to help you get better!

Examples:

Thank you, lungs, for making it possible for me to breathe each day.

Thank you, legs, for carrying me around and bringing me to different places.

Thank you, hands, for helping me hold stuff, write, and create.

Step 4. Focus on the Healing

After thanking your body, close your eyes again and picture your body glowing with a warm, healing light. Imagine this light traveling to any parts that are hurting or feeling tired or sore. As the light reaches the parts of your body that need some TLC, mentally say, "Thank you [body part] for doing your best to heal."

Step 5. Read or Share Your Notes

Once you have finished your love and gratitude notes, you can read them out loud to yourself. If you are feeling up to it, you might even want to share it with someone in your family. The important part is to really feel gratitude for your body and all the cool stuff it can do!

CHAPTER 5:
THE POWER OF SMALL THINGS

Life is full of big events and exciting moments, like birthdays, holidays, vacations, getting compliments, or getting an A on a test. These moments are great for sure, but you shouldn't forget to notice the smaller things that happen every day, too. After all, it is usually the little moments that build up to the big stuff, right?

Small Moments, Big Magic
Learning to appreciate the little things can bring you more happiness and help you feel more connected to the world around you. But what are these "little things?"

These are the small, everyday experiences that often go unnoticed. They aren't big or flashy, but they have this magical ability to brighten your day. Here are some examples:

- Enjoying a cool breeze on a hot day.
- Laughing at funny cat videos.
- Popcorn.
- A smile from a friend or crush in the hallway at school.
- Having a quiet moment with a good book.
- Movie night with family or friends.

These may be small moments, but when you start to really pay attention to them, you discover something cool. One, your day is FULL of these little moments. And two, if you string these little moments together, they give you non-stop cause for joy the whole day!

Now, the point of paying attention to little things is to give yourself plenty of opportunities to be grateful. Also, **when you take note of simple joys, you live more in the present moment rather than stressing about the past or future.** Yeah, that is something really weird about us humans.

We tend to worry a lot about things we missed, forgot, or did not do "right" *yesterday*. And if we are not doing that, we are probably fretting about what is going to happen *tomorrow*. If you think about it, it is kinda funny. It is like people are living in the past or future, but never just NOW.

Here is the good news—if you practice paying attention to small, happy moments happening RIGHT NOW, it pulls you out of your worries (past or future)! It helps you feel calm, centered, and more in control of your thoughts. And I have to tell you, feeling in control is a great feeling to have.

So, how do you get into the habit of noticing these "little things?" Here are some cool ideas for you! Try them all at least once and see which one you like best.

Use your senses. Look around you. What do you see, hear, feel, smell, or taste? Maybe it is the taste of your favorite snack or the soft feel of your pillow. Using your senses is not only great to start noticing the little things that bring you joy; it is also an awesome way to notice all sorts of things. For example, what your eyes appreciate (like a favorite fluffy sweater) might not be the same as what your ears can (like your favorite tunes).

Take breaks to reflect. Throughout the day, take a few moments to pause and think about what is going well. For example, the next time you pass a doorway, take a moment to look back at the room you are leaving. Anything cool happened there that you want to be grateful for? Or is there anything in there that makes you smile?

Keep a "Little Things" gratitude jar!

Step 1. Get a clear glass jar where you can store your gratitude notes. You will also need small pieces of paper in different colors and a pen or pencil. This will be your special gratitude jar, so feel free to decorate it in any way you like!

Step 2. At the end of each day, write down one to three little things that made you smile or happy. Write each small thing down on a small piece of paper, okay?

Step 3. Fold your paper and place it inside the jar. Over time, the jar will fill up with all the good things in your life!

When you are feeling down or having a tough day, open your jar and read some of your gratitude notes. It'll remind you of all the good things around you!

<u>Grateful Thoughts HIGHLIGHT More Reasons to Be Grateful</u>
When you start focusing on what you are grateful for, something amazing happens: you begin to notice even MORE things to be thankful for. It is like a

chain reaction! The more you think about the good stuff in your life, the more good things you see. Let's quickly break down how this works.

Having a grateful thought is like picking up a magnifying glass. Suddenly, you start noticing the small, often overlooked moments that brighten your day. With each thankful thought, your awareness of life's little blessings grows, revealing more and more reasons to feel grateful. Pretty cool, right?

Check out these examples:

- If you are thankful for your bestie, you will probably notice even more nice things they do for you, like sharing their lunch or making you laugh.
- If you are grateful for a sunny day, you might start appreciating how the sunshine feels on your skin or how it makes trees and flowers look bright and colorful.
- If you are grateful for your comfy bed, you begin to notice all the other cool stuff in your room.

And do you remember what we said about **neuroplasticity**? Gratitude helps rewire your brain. So, by focusing on these small moments, your brain starts to automatically look for MORE good things! Before you know it, you will be spotting reasons to feel grateful everywhere you look—with or without an actual magnifying glass.

Gratitude Creates a Positive Cycle

When you feel grateful, it not only helps you notice more positive things but also makes you feel better overall. It is this cool loop: the better you feel, the more good things you see, and the more good things you see, the better you feel!

Here is an example:

- You feel grateful for something small, like a **Get Well Soon** card from a friend.
- The thoughtfulness of the card makes you realize how lucky you are to have people who care about you.
- This warm feeling encourages you to reach out and thank your friend, strengthening your bond and making your friendship even stronger.
- As you express gratitude, you start to appreciate how supportive your entire circle is, and you feel wrapped in a big hug of love.
- Feeling supported lifts your mood, helping you focus on other good things in your life, like the comfort of your home or the warmth of a sunny day.
- This newfound positivity makes you more open to noticing small, joyful moments throughout the day—like how your siblings are trying not to annoy you when you have a headache or how your parents (or caregiver) are doing their best to help you recover.
- With each moment of gratitude, you start to feel even better physically and emotionally, boosting your overall sense of well-being.

This cycle keeps rolling. Every grateful thought leads to more positive feelings, which makes you more aware of the good around you, creating a continuous loop of happiness and appreciation. Boom!

Activity #5: Gratitude Mind Map

In this exercise, you will come up with your own gratitude cycle or chain reaction. By creating a visual representation of gratitude, you can see just how powerful ONE thankful thought can be. Dive right in!

Step 1. Start Your Gratitude Mind Map

Grab a blank piece of paper, a notebook, or a journal. Draw a large circle in the middle of the page and write down one thing you are grateful for today. This can be something simple, like "I am grateful for my dog" or "I am grateful for my comfy pajamas."

Around that circle, draw three more circles connected to it by lines (like a spider web). Now, think of three more things related to your first grateful thought.

For example, if you wrote, "I am grateful for my dog, Charlie," your three circles might say:

- Charlie makes me laugh.
- Charlie keeps me company when I am lonely.
- I love taking Charlie for walks.

Step 2. Expand Your Mind Map

Now, from each of those three circles, draw two more circles connected by lines. In each new circle, write down another reason why you are grateful based on the previous idea.

For example, from "Charlie makes me laugh," you might add:
- I feel happy when I laugh.

- Laughing puts me in a good mood for the rest of the day.

Keep going until you have at least two or three layers of circles connected to your original thought. This will show you how one grateful thought can grow into a whole chain of positive vibes!

Example:

Step 3. Reflect

After completing your drawing, take a moment to look at how many reasons to be grateful have grown from that one original thought. Is it not amazing how focusing on just one thing you are thankful for can lead to so many other positive thoughts?

Step 4. Share Your Gratitude Mind Map

When you are done, consider sharing your Gratitude Mind Map with someone. Why? It can intensify your happiness!

You see, when you share what makes you grateful and happy with someone, it reinforces those feelings within you, making them even more powerful. Plus, discussing positive things keeps the conversation focused on the good, extending those uplifting emotions and helping you stay in that positive, happy space for longer.

Feel free to share your Gratitude Mind Map with the person you are grateful for or with the person who contributed to that happy moment. You can also just share for the sake of sharing. For example, you can share with your family how happy and grateful you are about what a friend did for you.

CHAPTER 6:
THANKFULNESS FOR SUPPORT

One of the "bestest" ways to feel instant gratitude is to simply look around, notice, and appreciate the people who have your back. When you are ill or injured, it is easy to feel isolated. But if you look around, you will see that you are not alone at all. There are people who care about you and are stepping up to help in different ways!

So, **take a moment to think about the people who are there for you**. It might be a family member who checks in on you, a friend who sends a nice text, or even a neighbor who helps your parents out with running errands.

Maybe it is a kind doctor, a gentle nurse, or a supportive therapist guiding you through your recovery. Whoever they are, these people care about you, and their support is definitely something to really appreciate.

Sometimes, when we are struggling, it can be easy to miss these acts of kindness. You might feel too overwhelmed to see the help being offered. But pausing to recognize these gestures can shift your focus from what is hard to what is good and from what feels isolating to what feels supportive and connected.

Previously, we discussed how **gratitude has this magical and powerful way of making you feel all warm and happy inside, which then attracts even more positive vibes.**

When you are thankful for the support of others and express it, this is what happens: You feel good, they feel good, and the bond between you gets even stronger!

Think about it. When you do something nice, and the other person thanks you for it, doesn't it inspire you to keep on being kind and supportive? It is because you feel valued. You feel that your kindness is appreciated, so it motivates you to do more good. It is the same for people who support you.

When you express your appreciation, it often leads to more acts of support coming your way. It is like this awesome, positive cycle—the more you show gratitude, the more you invite love and care into your life. Simple. Beautiful. Magical.

By the way, being thankful really helps you be open to getting support from others. Like instead of thinking you are a burden, you start to see that people actually want to help you because they care. This mindset shift can make it easier to accept help, knowing it comes from a place of love.

Now, showing appreciation does not have to be complicated. Here are some easy-peasy ways to express your thanks:

- **Say Thank You.** A heartfelt "Thank You" already means a lot, whether you say it face-to-face, send a text, or jot it down in a note.

- **Acknowledge What They Do (or Did) for You.** Let people know that you see and appreciate their efforts in supporting you. For example, saying something like, "I know you are really busy with school projects and all, so

I really appreciate you taking the time to check in on me" can go a long way.

- **Give Back.** If you are feeling up to it, a small gesture like offering to help in return can really show your appreciation. It does not have to be big—just a little something to let them know you appreciate what they did.

  For example, you can offer to listen when they need to talk about something or help with a simple task when you feel better. Even a small gesture, like making them a cup of tea or sharing a kind word, can show how much their support means to you.

- **Ask How THEY are Feeling.** Just as they often check in on you, make sure to ask how they are feeling as well. A simple "How are you?" or "Are you okay?" lets them know you care about them as much as they care about you!

- **Share Your Positive Vibe!** If you are in a great mood or have something awesome to share, make sure to tell them! Your smiles, laughs, and stories of appreciation can really boost their mood and show them that their support helps with your healing.

- **Be Patient and Compassionate.** Sometimes, when you are sick or injured your patience can be on the "thin side." Like you might find it super annoying when people constantly ask how you are doing or keep on trying to push their positive vibes on you. But you know what? It is way, way, way better to be grateful that there are people who care about you, than to feel alone and think that no one cares, right?

It can also be that you notice that the people around you are not in the mood one day. They might take long to respond to you, or they seem focused on something or someone else.

During these times, remember to show patience and kindness. They might be having a bad day or they might just be really tired, and you showing *your support* can be just the thing they need. After all, kindness and understanding go both ways, right?

Activity #6: Gratitude Letter

Writing a gratitude letter is probably one of the most powerful ways to show your appreciation for someone who has supported you. So, whenever you want to say more than just two words (Thank You), try this activity!

Step 1. Select Who You Want to Thank

Think of someone who has supported you during a tough time. It could be a family member, friend, healthcare provider, or anyone who has been there for you.

Step 2. Reflect on the Support You Received

Take a few minutes to think about how this person has helped you. What did they do for you? How did their support make you feel? This helps you connect with the true value of their kindness.

Step 3. Start Your Letter

Begin with a greeting like "Dear [Name]" or "Hi [Name]," and then let them know why you are writing. You can start with something simple like, "Just wanted to take a minute to thank you for your support."

Step 4. Be Specific

Next, mention *specific things* they did that meant a lot to you. Whether it was a kind word, a thoughtful gesture, or just being there when you needed them, including details shows that you have noticed and appreciated their efforts.

Example: Thanks for hanging out with me this past month; I really appreciated those visits.

Step 5. Share How It Helped You

Explain how their support made a difference for you. Did it boost your hope? Did it help you get through a tough day? Let them know the impact they had.

Example: I gotta say there were times when I was really feeling sad and lonely. But your visits totally brightened my mood and made me feel like I was still part of our group, even if I cannot be physically there with you guys... yet!

Step 6. Close with Gratitude

Wrap up your letter with a heartfelt thank you. You can also mention that you value the relationship and look forward to staying in touch.

Example: Anyway, thanks again for hanging out with me. (Those double chocolate chip cookies are appreciated, too!) I feel lucky to have you as my friend, and I appreciate your kindness and care. Talk soon!

Step 7. Deliver Your Letter

Once you have written your letter, think about the best way to share it. You can give it to the person directly, send it in the mail (old school but very thoughtful!), or even read it out loud to them. No matter how you deliver it, I promise that your words will have a lasting impact.

CHAPTER 7:
FINDING GRATITUDE WHEN SICK

I get it. When you are not feeling your best, it can be challenging to stay positive. But finding gratitude, even when you are sick or injured, can make those tough days a little easier. So let me help you find things to be thankful for, even when it is hard, okay?

Ways to Discover Gratitude

Be Thankful for What is Working
Even if one part of your body is not feeling great, other parts are still strong and ready to go. So, think about the things your body can still do—whether it is your hands that can draw, your mind that can think, or your eyes that can read.

Example:
My leg might hurt, but I am thankful my arms can still play video games!

Focus on Small Comforts
During hard days, it is important to appreciate the little things that bring comfort. Maybe it is a cozy blanket, binge-watching your favorite TV show, or a pet snuggling with you. These small comforts can make a big difference in how you feel.

Example:
I am grateful for my favorite pillow because it is comfortable, soft and helps me rest.

Find Gratitude in Rest

Being ill or injured means your body needs rest to heal. While it might feel frustrating and boring, you can find gratitude in the opportunity to slow down, rest, and let your body do its thing. Rest is your body's way of getting stronger.

Example:
I am thankful for the chance to rest so my body can recover.

Appreciate Your Strength Each Day

When you are not feeling well, just getting through each day can be a superhero act! Recognize and be grateful for your ability to KEEP GOING, even on the hardest days. Each day you manage to push through discomfort, you are showing resilience and courage, and that is something to be proud of.

Example:
I am thankful for my strength for getting through today, even though it was not easy.

Be Grateful for the Lessons in Patience

Illness or injury often teaches us patience—whether we like it or not! While it is tough to wait for your body to heal, this "downtime" can teach you to slow down, listen to your body, and just trust the process. Finding gratitude for the lesson of patience can help make the recovery easier to handle.

Example: I am grateful for the patience I am gaining while my body heals in its own time.

Remember Better Days

Think about the times when you were healthy, having fun, and doing things you love—not because they are gone, but because you experienced them. Remembering these good times can help you inspire hope that better days will come again. It is a reminder that this tough time won't last forever.

Example:
I am grateful for that fun day at the park last month. I am looking forward to having even more fun days when I am better.

Self-Compassion: It Is Okay to Feel Down Sometimes

When you are sick or injured, it is natural to feel frustrated, sad, or even a little angry. You might wish you could do more or just feel better as soon as possible. These feelings are completely normal, and it is important to remember that being tough on yourself won't make things easier. This is where **self-compassion** comes in.

Self-compassion means being kind to yourself when things get rough, just like you would be kind to a friend who is having a hard time.

Now, this is really important: **Feeling upset, frustrated, or sad during hard times doesn't mean you are weak**. Everyone has bad days, and it is perfectly normal to experience those emotions when you are not feeling your best. The key is to be cool with those emotions without judging yourself for having them. It is 100% okay to admit when you are struggling.

So, **how do you practice self-compassion**?

First, **do not push your emotions away**. You have to recognize what you are feeling for what it is. It is okay to say, "I am feeling sad," or "I am frustrated that I cannot be outside and hang with my friends," or "Being sick sucks!" Being honest about your feelings is an important part of healing.

Second, **be kind to yourself**. When you are feeling low, remind yourself that it is okay to take it easy. You do not have to be perfect or strong all the time. Say something kind to yourself, like "It is okay to feel this way" or "I am doing my best right now."

Next, **give yourself a break**. Sometimes, the best way to show self-compassion is to give yourself a break and chillax. Your body is working hard to heal, and resting is part of that process. So, instead of feeling guilty for resting or being annoyed for "doing nothing," recognize that you are giving your body what it needs.

Lastly, **go ahead and reach out for support**. Here is another funny thing we humans do: We always tell people to call us when they need help. We might even say, "I am always here for you." But when it is the other way around (we are the ones who need help), we hold back.

You DO NOT have to go through hard times alone. Self-compassion also means letting yourself ask for help or comfort when you need it. So, go ahead—chat with a family member, a friend, or someone you trust about what you are feeling. Remember, everyone goes through tough times, and it is okay to be kind and patient with yourself as you work through them.

Activity #7: Gratitude Stone

This activity is a cool way to find things to be grateful for during tough times. Here is how it works:

Step 1. Find Your Gratitude Stone

Go on a hunt for a small, smooth rock that feels nice in your hand. You can look for it at the park, on the beach, in your garden, etc. If a rock is not your thing, you can use a shell or even a small gemstone. Whatever it is, put it on your bedside table.

Step 2. Set Your Intention

Every night before sleeping, hold the stone in your hand and think back on your day. Focus on one thing, no matter how small, that you are grateful for. It can be anything—feeling less pain, getting a message from a friend, or just enjoying a quiet moment.

Step 3. Express Your Gratitude

As you hold the stone, say to yourself, "I am thankful for [what you are grateful for]." Let the feeling of gratitude wash over you for a few moments. This simple act of holding the rock and thinking about what went well during the day can really help you end the day on a high note!

Step 4. Create a Routine

Try to make this a nightly thing, okay? No matter how tough the day was, hold your rock and find something to be thankful for. Even the smallest joy or comfort will help shift your mindset toward gratitude and hope.

CHAPTER 8:
FROM BAD DAYS TO BETTER DAYS

Accepting and Releasing Unhelpful Thoughts and Feelings

Everyone has tough days. Whether you are feeling sick, tired, or upset, it is normal to have days when everything feels just a little too much. When you are having a rough day, it is easy for negative thoughts to sneak into your mind.

Maybe you are thinking things like, "I will never feel better," or "Why is this happening to me? It is so unfair!" Sadly, these thoughts can make you feel even worse. But here is something important to remember: **It is okay to feel like that sometimes, but you do not have to hold on to these thoughts and feelings!** Instead, feel them and release them.

When you are feeling low, accept those negative thoughts instead of trying to push them away. If you accept them, it is like giving yourself permission to feel sad, angry, or frustrated.

Once you acknowledge those feelings, the next thing to do is let them go. Keeping negative thoughts around can really weigh you down, almost like lugging around a backpack stuffed with rocks. The more you hold on to them, the heavier they become. But if you let them go, it feels like taking the backpack off and feeling lighter again.

Accepting and releasing negative thoughts is like clearing the dark clouds in your mind so you can see the sunshine again. And a really cool way to do this is by trying out a fun and creative activity called **Balloon Release** on the next page.

Activity #8: Balloon Release

This activity helps you recognize and accept negative thoughts and feelings and then let them go in a way that feels light and freeing—just like letting go of a balloon and watching it float away into the sky.

What you will need:
- a few sheets of paper (you can use colored paper if you want)
- markers, crayons, or colored pencil
- a pair of scissors (make sure to ask an adult for help if you need it)

Step 1. Draw or Cut Out Balloons

Draw a few simple balloon shapes on your paper. You can make as many balloons as you like—maybe three or four to start. Next, carefully cut out your balloon shapes. Each balloon stands for a negative thought or feeling that is bothering you.

Step 2. Write Down Any Unhelpful Thoughts and Feelings

Take a balloon and write down a thought or feeling that has been bothering you. It could be something like, "I am feeling super frustrated today," or "I am scared I will not get better." Now, just be real with yourself about what you are feeling—it is okay to put it all out there!

Step 3. Imagine Letting Go

Now that you have written down your unhelpful thoughts and feelings imagine that these balloons are real. Picture yourself holding the string of each balloon. In your mind, look at the balloon and think about saying something like one of these options:

- I accept that I am having this unhelpful thought right now, but I am ready to move on from it.
- I am feeling _____, but I am letting this feeling go.
- I am having the negative thought that _____, but you know what? I am just going to let it go now.

Step 4. Release the Balloons

After you have imagined letting go, rip each balloon shape into small pieces. This symbolizes releasing the negative thoughts from your mind. As you tear each one up, take a deep breath and imagine yourself feeling lighter and happier.

Optional: Hey, do you have any real, unused balloons at home? Maybe some leftover balloons from a birthday party? If you do, blow them up and think about putting all your frustrations inside it. Like each time you blow air into the balloon, imagine blowing each unhelpful thought and feeling inside. Next, tie the balloon up and let it go!

Pop it (safely; make sure an adult is around), or let the air out slowly. As the air escapes from the balloon, imagine your negative thoughts leaving too. This can be a fun and powerful way to let go of heavy and unhelpful thoughts and feelings that are weighing you down.

Changing Negative Thoughts and Feelings to Positive Ones

After releasing unhelpful thoughts and emotions, the next thing to do is figure out how to shift your vibe to a positive one. Hmmm, how do you pull that off?

Think of your emotions like colors. Sometimes, you might be feeling "blue" (sad) or "red" (angry). Just like you can mix and change colors on a paint palette, you can totally shift your emotions too! You can take negative thoughts and feelings and gently move them toward something brighter and more uplifting.

For example, say that you are having an unhelpful thought today, like, "I am recovering too slowly. Will I ever recover at all?!" I am sure a thought like this is totally bringing you down and making you feel pretty sad, right? But just like what we talked about earlier, it is all about accepting them and then letting them go.

So, accept the fact that you are feeling a bit down today, and then release that thought by saying, "I release you!" out loud or doing the **Balloon Release** activity on the previous page.

Next, think about ways to turn your thoughts and emotions around. For example, if you are feeling angry, what can you do to feel calmer? If you are feeling down, what thoughts can you focus on that will bring a smile to your face and lift your spirits? By shifting your focus, you are helping yourself move on from those heavier emotions and embrace the brighter, happier ones.

To help you with this, we are going to do a fun activity called the **Emotion Wheel**!

Activity #9: Emotion Wheel

This activity is all about understanding your feelings and finding ways to turn those negative vibes into something more positive. Are you all set? Come on, let's do this!

Step 1. Identify How You are Feeling

Check out the Emotion Wheel below. Think about how you are feeling right now and find the section that matches your emotion.

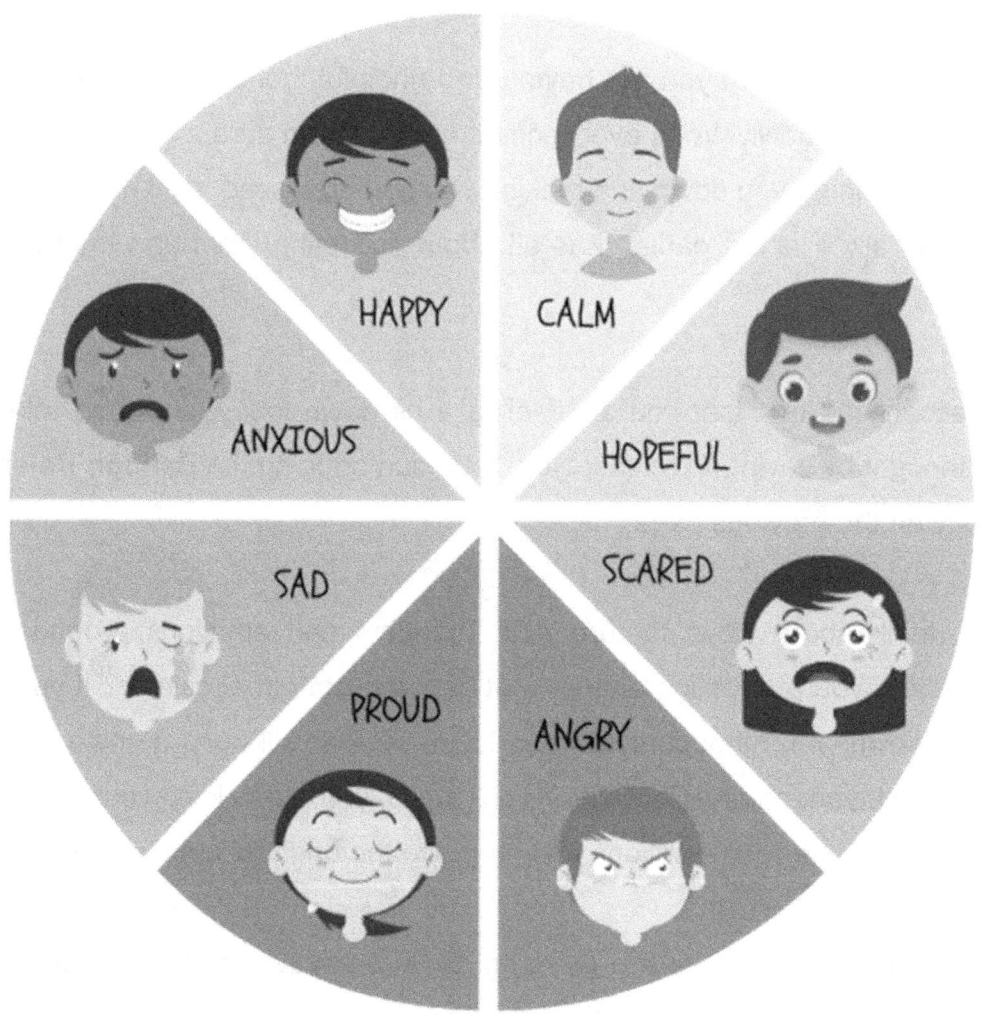

Step 2. Pick a Positive Vibe

After identifying what you are feeling, think about how you want to feel instead. Look at the positive emotions on the wheel—like "green" for happy or "yellow" for calm. Pick one of these emotions and focus on it.

Step 3. Change It Up, Change It Up, Change It Up

After you pick a positive emotion, think about something that makes you feel that way. For example, if you chose "happy," bring to mind a fun memory, a favorite hobby that gives you joy, or something nice that someone did for you lately. If you chose "calm," find a spot where you chill by yourself for a bit and just take some deep breaths.

Take a moment to really think about the vibe you want to feel, and let that good energy push away any of the negative stuff you were dealing with at the start of this exercise.

Step 4. Reflect on How You Feel Now

Once you have spent some time on those good vibes, pause for a sec and check in with yourself. Do you notice a shift in your emotions? Hey, even if it is just a little change, that is an awesome start!

Part 3: The Law of Attraction for Healing

CHAPTER 9:

THE LAW OF ATTRACTION -

THE MAGIC POWER OF FOCUS AND INTENTION

Hey, have you ever stared at something for a long time, like a small pebble or a flower or the moon up in the sky at night, and noticed that it started to look... bigger?! It might even start to feel like it is the only thing you can see. Why is that?

When you focus on something, your brain makes it seem larger and more important than everything else around you. This is like a superpower you have: the power of **focus** and **intention**.

Just like how staring at something can make it seem bigger, focusing your thoughts and feelings on something you want in life can help bring more of it into your world. Super cool, right? This is the magic of the **Law of Attraction**.

Maybe you have even heard adults say things like "what you focus on grows" or "what you think about comes about." Again, this is pretty much how the Law of Attraction works. It means that **your thoughts and attention have power**.

Whatever you set your mind on—whatever you think about and focus on the most—that is what you attract into your life.

Imagine your thoughts like a big, powerful life magnet. When you think positive, hopeful, or happy thoughts, you attract positive experiences. But when you focus on negative thoughts or worries, it is like you are pulling more of that into your life. That is not cool!

If gratitude is all about being thankful for what you already have in your life, then the Law of Attraction is about concentrating on what you want to have. It is an awesome way of using your mind to bring great things into your life.

Gratitude = Being grateful for <u>what you have</u>.
Law of Attraction = Focusing on <u>what you want</u>.

In other words, what you put out into the world with your thoughts and vibe is what comes back to you. Just like a boomerang, you know? The energy you send out to the universe is what comes back to you.

That is why it is super important to concentrate on the things you want to happen (like healing) and not the things you are afraid of or do not want to happen (like staying sick). You are in control of your thoughts, and by using the power of the Law of Attraction, you can bring more of the good stuff into your life!

Now, you may think that the Law of Attraction is just some funny, magic stuff, but it is actually connected to something scientists call the **placebo effect**.

A *placebo* is something that looks like real medicine, but it does not have any actual medicine in it at all. And yet, people get better from taking them. Some studies even show that placebos are 50% as effective as real medicine![5]

The placebo effect is when people start feeling better because they BELIEVE they will, even if they did not actually take any real medicine. This is an awesome example of how powerful the mind can be.

Your thoughts can influence how you feel emotionally and physically. So, if you believe that good things like healing are coming your way, you are more likely to "grow" or "attract" into your life.

Important: Your mind is super powerful, and there is zero doubt it is important for your healing. But it is still super important to take any real medicine your doctor prescribes. Think of it this way: **Doctors prescribe "body medicine,"** which is the stuff that helps your body get better. **The Law of Attraction is about "energy medicine,"** which is the vibes you put out there to bring about what you think about! (Mind-body connection, remember?)

How Does the Law of Attraction Work?

The Law of Attraction is kind of like planting a seed. When you plant a seed in the ground, you water it, give it sunlight, and take care of it. Over time, it grows into a big, healthy plant. The same goes for your thoughts!

When you focus on what you want—like feeling better and completely bouncing back from your illness or injury—you are planting a "thought seed." And the more you focus on that thought, the more it grows into something real.

But remember, you cannot just plant a seed in the ground and walk away. **You have to keep focusing on it, thinking positively about it, believing in it, and taking little steps to make it happen**. That is what makes the Law of Attraction work—it is about intention, focus, and the actions you take.

Here is how you can use the Law of Attraction to get what you want:

Step 1. Figure Out What You Really Want (Intention)
First, think about what you want to attract. This is your **intention**—what you want to focus on. Now, be as supper clear and complete as possible about what you want. The universe does not like to guess these things. It wants to know EXACTLY what you want.

So, do not just say, "I will feel better." Say, "I will recover from my broken ankle completely. Like 100%. I will be able to walk without crutches in two months and start joining my dad for morning jogs in three months."

And here's something even better: Set your intention in the *present tense*, "I have recovered completely from my broken ankle. I am able to walk without crutches and join my dad for morning jogs."

Why is setting your intention in the present tense better? You see, in the context of the Law of Attraction, using the *present tense* aligns your thoughts and feelings with the reality you desire as if it is happening now.

Thinking or speaking this way communicates to your subconscious mind that what you want is already yours. Essentially, it shifts your mindset from a state of "wanting" (which focuses on what you do not have) to a state of "having" (which focuses on abundance and fulfillment).

Now, have a really good think and set your intention below:

_____
_____
_____
_____

Step 2. Picture Your Intention As If It Already Happened

After setting your intention (in the present tense), spend some time imagining or visualizing it. That is, picture yourself doing exactly what you intended. Using the example above, this would mean imagining yourself walking to the living room without crutches, lightly jogging with your dad, and feeling the sunshine on your face, your sweat dripping lightly, and so on.

This is what we call **visualization,** and the clearer and more detailed you make it, the better it works! Visualization is like watering and giving sunlight to your ideas—it helps them thrive.

Step 3. Believe. Believe. Believe.

You have to totally believe that what you want to happen can actually happen. This is a super important step in the Law of Attraction. If you do not 100% believe in it, it is like planting your "thought seed" and then forgetting to take care of it. As a result, your plant will not grow. ☹ So, you gotta trust that what you are focusing on will come true.

You know, when my little Emma was sick with leukemia... I believed with ALL MY HEART that she would get better. Every morning, I would say, "Thank you for her healing." And in my mind, she was not just going to be healed. She was already healed! So, dearest young reader, BELIEVE!

Step 4. Take Action

The Law of Attraction is not wishful thinking. It is positive thinking + taking action. 👊

You cannot just think about what you want and then do nothing. Actions show that you are serious about your intention. So, if you want to do better in school, start studying a little more. If you want to make a new friend, be friendly and smile at people. If you want to get better, do anything and everything that will help speed up your recovery, like:

- **Eat well.** Fuel your body with good foods so it can bounce back quicker.
- **Sleep well.** Rest gives your body time to repair and recover.
- **Take your meds.** Following what your doctor says is key to healing.
- **Hobbies!** Do things you enjoy to lift your spirits and keep your mind positive.
- **Laugh!** Laughing can totally lift your spirits and help your body release those feel-good hormones.
- **De-stress your body.** Give deep breathing a shot, maybe some light stretches, or even try meditating to help you chill out and concentrate on feeling better.

Step 5. Let It Go

Once you have set your intention, visualized it, believed it, and taken action… let go of any worries! Do not stress about when or how it is going to happen. Trust that the Law of Attraction magnet is working and that your thoughts and actions are attracting exactly what you want. Relax and let the universe take care of the rest!

Hey, just a heads up, the Law of Attraction works both ways. If you spend too much time worrying about something or thinking about things you do not want, you might accidentally attract those things into your life. Uh-oh. That is why it is really important to focus on positive thoughts, even when things are not exactly going that way.

So, if you ever find yourself having an unhelpful or negative thought or emotion, feel them and release them. Just like what you learned in the previous chapter.

CHAPTER 10:
ATTRACTING PHYSICAL HEALING

I am sure there are days when you wish that your body could heal faster. That is okay. It is a perfectly normal wish to have. But you know, the Law of Attraction is all about keeping your mind on the good things and really believing that they are already happening.

So, instead of thinking something like, "I wish I could heal faster," how about we change that thought frequency to, "Amazing! My body is healing faster every day." Can you feel the difference in the energy level there? Awesome, isn't it?

One of the best ways to use the Law of Attraction for healing is by imagining your body getting stronger and healthier every single day. Go ahead, close your eyes for a moment, and picture yourself as healthy and strong as you can be, better even than before you got sick or injured.

Imagine waking up with your body full of healing energy. Imagine all the awesome stuff you will get to do when you are feeling better, like hanging out with your friends outside, diving back into your favorite hobbies, or just enjoying life and feeling good.

This kind of imagination is more than just daydreaming; it is called **manifesting**. When you imagine yourself getting better, it tells your body that it is time to heal and go all in! It is like giving yourself a pep talk, saying, "You have got this. Keep going! You are doing great!" And you know what? Your body totally responds to those good vibes by speeding up your healing.

So, every day, take a few minutes to imagine yourself feeling a little stronger. Maybe picture the cells in your body as little warriors battling sickness or how your muscles are getting tougher after an injury. The more you work on visualizing this, the better your body will get at it.

Pay Attention to Small Signs of Improvement

Healing does not happen all at once, so it is important to notice all the little signs that show you are getting better. Maybe one day, you notice that your headache is not as bad as it was the day before. Or maybe you are able to walk a little farther without feeling as tired.

So, every morning, I want you to do a super quick "feel-good body scan." Just quickly go over your body and give it small compliments. For example, suppose you injured your shoulder; you can say something like this:

Thanks, eyes, for waking up and letting me see my comfy room right away.
Thanks, nose, for picking up on the smell of pancakes from the kitchen.
Thanks, shoulder, for going overtime on the healing while I slept.
Gotta go to the bathroom now; thanks, legs!

Throughout the day, keep an eye out for more signs of progress, like, "Awesome! I walked farther than I did yesterday."

Each time you notice these small healing moments do a little mental dance of joy. The more positive you feel about your progress, the more you attract even better results!

Release Your Fears

When you are sick or injured, feeling scared is normal. You might worry about when you will get better or whether things will go back to normal. But these kinds of thoughts can make you feel stuck, and they might even slow down your healing. That is because fear and worry use up A LOT of your energy. When you let fear take over, your body ends up putting in extra effort to heal.

Now, the cool thing about the Law of Attraction is that you can **let go of your fears and swap them out for hope**. When you have hope, it helps your body relax and focus on getting better. So, yeah, hope totally beats fear any day. Booyah!

But first, like what I always say, **feel and release**, okay? I do not want you to feel bad or discouraged when you get a little scared or worried. Just say, "Ah, there you are, Mr. Fear. You entered my mind again. But I will let you go now because Ms. Hope is here."

Next, shift and say to yourself:

I trust that my body is healing.
Each day, I am getting better and stronger.
I 100% believe I can beat this!
I see myself fully healed and doing _____.
I see myself fully healed and doing _____.
I see myself fully healed and doing _____.
I see myself fully healed and doing _____.
I see myself fully healed and doing _____.

Activity #10: Healing Visualization Journal

This exercise will help you focus your thoughts on getting better and keep track of your progress. It is a cool way to mix creativity, thankfulness, and good vibes!

Step 1. Find a Quiet Place

This is your special time to focus on your healing, so find a quiet and comfortable space to sit. You can sit on your bed, on a chair, or anywhere you feel relaxed. Close your eyes and take a few deep breaths to help you calm your mind and body.

Step 2. Visualize Your Healing

Close your eyes and imagine your body healing. Picture yourself feeling stronger and healthier each day. You can visualize the parts of your body that need healing like your muscles getting stronger or your immune system fighting off illness.

Picture a bright, glowing healing light traveling inside your body and gently direct it to where you want healing to happen. For example, if you broke your leg, imagine the light zooming in on your leg and repairing it. If your immune system is taking a hit, breathe deeply. And as you exhale, imagine the light shining brighter inside you, driving away the illness out of your body.

Step 3. Reflect in Your Journal

After you have spent some time visualizing your healing, open your journal. You can write down what you imagined, or you can draw it. Write about how your body is getting stronger and healthier. You can also write about any small signs of improvement you noticed that day. If you are not sure what to write, start with something like:

My body is working hard to help me recover.

I noticed that I felt better when I was not out of breath after my walk.

Step 4. Practice Daily

Make this exercise a part of your daily routine. You really do not have to put in a ton of time—just a few minutes each day will do the trick. Remember, the more you focus on positive thoughts and healing, the more your body will respond.

CHAPTER 11:
ATTRACTING EMOTIONAL STRENGTH

Resilience is your ability to bounce back when things get tough. It means that even when you feel sad, frustrated, or in pain, you can find a way to push through it and feel strong again. Think of resilience like a tree that bends like crazy during a strong storm. Strong winds may push it this way and that way, but it just bends and stays strong—it does not break.

The cool thing about resilience is that it is a special kind of strength. It does not come from the muscles on your arms—it comes from inside you. (Yep, mind muscles!)

When you are unwell, resilience helps you handle being ill. Now, it does not mean you never feel upset about being sick. Instead, it means that you trust yourself. You believe that you can deal with being ill and everything that goes with it—and get back on your feet.

It is like being a superhero, really. Superheroes are not superheroes because they avoid villains and danger, right? Superheroes are superheroes because they know that villains and danger are out there—but they face them head-on anyway and bounce back stronger.

So, there's something else to consider about resilience. This mind-muscle works just like any other muscle you have in your body. The more you use it, the better it becomes!

Now, you might wonder, "What does the Law of Attraction have to do with resilience?" Well, the Law of Attraction is all about focusing on what you want to happen, right? If you combine resilience with the Law of Attraction, you are creating an amazing superpower combo right there. How?

Do you remember what I said about the Law of Attraction needing total belief? For the Law of Attraction to work, you gotta believe that what you want can and will happen. Well, resilience helps with that confidence.

Think of it like this: If you are resilient, it is like you are saying, "I got this." When you practice the Law of Attraction, you are saying, "Not only have I got this, but I can attract even more amazing things into my life." Boom!

Activity #11: Resilience Shield

Let's create a **Resilience Shield** to help you focus on your inner strength and protect yourself from negative thoughts. This shield is a reminder of all the things that help you feel strong, no matter what challenges come your way.

Step 1. Imagine Your Shield

Close your eyes and imagine a shield that protects you. This shield is filled with everything that makes you feel strong, safe, and happy when things get hard.

Step 2. Add Your Support

Think about the people who are there for you, lift you up, and help you feel strong. This could be family members, friends, teachers, or anyone who supports you when things get tough. These people are a part of your shield.

These are the people on my shield:

_____
_____
_____
_____

Step 3. Add Your Strengths

Now, think about the strengths you have inside. What are the qualities that make you resilient? Are you brave? Kind? Patient? Creative? These inner strengths are what help you get through tough times, and they are a big part of your shield.

These are the strengths on my shield:

_____
_____
_____
_____

Step 4. Add Activities That Make You Feel Good

Next, think about the activities that make you feel better when you are having a hard time. This could be cuddling a pet, reading a favorite book, or spending time outdoors. These activities are part of your shield, too, because they help you feel happier and more positive.

These are the "feel-good activities" on my shield:

_____
_____
_____
_____

Step 5. Add a Few "Feel Good" Statements

Now that you have thought about the people, strengths, and activities that make you strong, it is time to add a few confidence-boosting statements that help you stay focused on your strengths. This could be something like, "I am strong and can handle anything" or "I have the power to bounce back."

These are the feel-good statements on my shield:

_____
_____
_____

_____

_____

Take a moment to think about everything that makes up your Resilience Shield—the people, the strengths, the activities, and your affirmation. Whenever you are feeling down, remember these things to help you feel stronger and more positive.

Cool idea: Grab some pens, markers, crayons, stickers—whatever you like! And do not forget a big piece of colored paper. Follow the steps above to make a cool Resilience Shield that you can cut out and hang on a wall in your room.

CHAPTER 12:
AFFIRMATIONS: POSITIVE STATEMENTS FOR HEALING

Affirmations are simple, positive statements that you tell yourself. They encourage you to believe in yourself and the things you want to achieve. When you say an affirmation, you are tuning into some really good energy.

Check out these examples of affirmations you may want to say about yourself. Feel free to check which ones you want to say from this moment on or add new ones to the list.

[ ] I am resilient.
[ ] I am strong and capable.
[ ] I can handle any challenge that comes my way.
[ ] I am smart and love learning new things.
[ ] I am kind to myself and others.
[ ] I am proud of who I am.
[ ] I can make today a great day.
[ ] I am brave, even when things are hard.
[ ] I am a good friend, and I care about others.
[ ] I can achieve anything I set my mind to.
[ ] Others:

_____
_____
_____
_____

Don't these affirmations make you feel good, strong, and confident? Don't they pump up your energy and make you feel all positive and hopeful? Of course they do!

Now, the following are affirmations you may want to say about your healing. Feel free to check which ones you want to say from this moment on or add new ones to the list.

[ ] My body is healing.
[ ] I am getting stronger and healthier every day.
[ ] I trust in my body's ability to recover.
[ ] Each day brings me closer to full health.
[ ] I am patient with my healing process.
[ ] My mind is calm, and my body is healing.
[ ] I feel super energized and full of life!
[ ] I am grateful for my body's strength.
[ ] I release all stress and embrace healing.
[ ] My body and mind are totally in sync right now, working hard to get me back to feeling my best.
[ ] Others:

_____
_____
_____
_____

Don't these healing affirmations make you feel healthier already?!

Now, the cool thing about affirmations is that they can change the way you think. Do you remember our discussion about *neuroplasticity*? Your brain is flexible and can form new habits and ways of thinking.

So, if you say any of the above affirmations over and over and over again, your brain will start to take them seriously! And what your brain believes, the body will start to believe too![6,7]

Activity #12: Healing Affirmation Mirror

This exercise is called the **Healing Affirmation Mirror** because you will be saying affirmations while looking at yourself in the mirror. It might seem a bit weird at the start, but trust me, the more you do it, the more powerful it becomes!

Step 1. Find a Mirror

Look for a mirror in your room or anywhere else in your home where you can get a good look at yourself. This is the spot for you to say your healing affirmations. It is important to look at yourself while saying the affirmations because it is all about connection, you know?

Step 2. Choose Your Healing Affirmation

Think about what you want for your body's healing. Choose a positive statement (affirmation) that focuses on your recovery. Remember to be as clear and detailed as you can be. For example, you might say, "My head wound is healing quickly and smoothly, and each day, I feel less pain and more strength."

My healing affirmation is:

_____

_____

Step 3. Look Yourself in the Mirror

Stand tall, look into your eyes, and say your healing affirmation out loud. Say it three to five times. Speak clearly and BELIEVE in what you are saying. Remember, the more you repeat it, the more your mind will start to accept it as true.

Step 4. Smile and Breathe

After saying your affirmation, take a deep breath and smile at yourself. Smiling helps you feel even more positive and relaxed, which is good for your healing.

Step 5. Repeat Daily

Practice this healing affirmation exercise every day, either in the morning or before bed. If you include this in your daily routine, it will help your body get stronger and healthier over time.

CHAPTER 13:
VISION BOARDS: SEEING YOUR FUTURE HEALTHY SELF

A **vision board** is a collection of pictures, words, and things that represent your goals, dreams, and how you want to see yourself in the future. Think of it this way: If you could snap a photo of yourself in your best or happiest moment in, let us say, 30 days, 3 months, 1 year, or maybe even 3 years down the road, what would that picture look like?

Vision boards are a cool way to help you focus on what you want to achieve by creating a visual reminder that you can look at every single day. The idea behind a vision board is that by focusing on these images and goals, you can attract them into your life—exactly how the Law of Attraction works!

For example, if you want to recover fast from illness or injury, here are some of the things you might want to place on your vision board.

- Pictures of people being active (or a snapshot of you being active and healthy before getting sick).
- Images of your favorite sports.
- Your favorite healthy meals and snacks.
- Pictures of water reminding you to stay hydrated.
- Words like "strength," "energy," or "great health."
- Nature scenes that make you feel peaceful.
- Inspirational quotes about healing.
- A super big and smiling emoji to remind you to stay positive.
- Photos of cool places you want to visit when you are feeling better.

- A picture of a happy moment you cannot wait to experience once you feel better. (This does not have to be something "big." I remember a vision board I saw a few years ago where a child who was sick with digestive issues put a picture of a tall glass of ice-cold pineapple juice!)

Basically, every time you look at your vision board, you should be reminded of what you want... no, hold up, of what you are going to achieve!

Think of vision boards as "appointments with destiny" or "appointments with your future self." Now, remember, the Law of Attraction works best when you believe 100% that what you want *can* and *will* happen. So, when you look at your vision board, be in **believing mode** rather than wishing mode. That is, visualize and feel as if your goals are already happening!

Important: Vision boards are not just about collecting material things. Of course, you can include pictures of stuff you want to have, but make sure that you also include pictures of what you want to *experience*.

That is why it is super important for your vision board to show how you want to *feel* in the future. Whether it is feeling healthy, strong, or happy, your vision board should represent both the stuff that you want to have and the positive emotions you want to experience along the way.

Also, your dreams and goals can change over time. What you add to your vision board now might not be what you want in a few weeks, months, or years, and that is totally fine too. Make the changes you want, whenever you want. You are the boss!

Lastly, vision boards are not about perfection. If there is anything you are unsure about, that is okay. There is no rush. Honestly, I think it would be awesome for you to take your time and turn making a vision board into a fun project.

Activity #13: Healing Vision Board

In this exercise, you will create a **Healing Vision Board** that highlights your journey to feeling better and getting healthier.

Step 1. Gather Your Materials

Firstly, decide what type of board you want to use. You can use a big white cardboard, a corkboard, or even a large sheet of paper like a poster board or craft paper.

Next, grab some magazines, and old pictures or albums, and a pair of scissors. You will also need materials to attach items to your board, such as glue, tape, tacks, or cork pins (if you are using a cork board).

Lastly, unleash your creativity by having crayons, markers, stickers, and other decorative items on hand.

Step 2. Think About Your Health Goals

Take a few moments to think about what you want to happen and how you want to feel. Do you want more energy? Do you want to feel stronger? Try to be as clear and specific as you can with your health goals.

Step 3. Choose Images and Words for Your Board

Look through your magazines and pictures and find images and words that represent health and healing. For example, you can cut out pictures of healthy foods, people exercising, nature scenes, or anything that makes you feel good. You can also print images from the internet that represent healing, strength, and health—whatever works for you. Also, do not forget to add words like "strength," "energy," or "healing" on your board. Choose whatever makes you feel inspired!

Step 4. Arrange and Attach Your Images

Once you have all your images and words, arrange them on your board in a way that looks good to you, and then attach them. There is no right or wrong way to do this—just make it your own.

Step 5. Place Your Board Somewhere You Can See It

Hang your vision board somewhere you will see it every day—on your bedroom wall, close to your desk, or anywhere that keeps your health goals front and center. Every time you see it, just picture how awesome it is going to feel when you're healthy and strong. During tough days, look at your board for motivation.

Nothing's Happening… Nothing's Happening!

It takes time for the ideas on your vision board to turn into real-life stuff. But patience is key—it takes time for your goals to manifest. If you are feeling discouraged, here are two things you can do:

- **Ensure you believe 100%.** Take a moment to check in with yourself. Do you truly believe that your vision will come true? Sometimes doubt sneaks in, so refocus on positive, confident thoughts!

- **Expand your vision board.** Add new images or words that support your goals. This boosts your energy and reinforces your confidence in what you want to accomplish. It also reminds you that your journey is *ongoing*.

CHAPTER 14:
BELIEVING AND STAYING POSITIVE DURING TOUGH DAYS

Sometimes, it can be difficult to stay positive when you are ill or during days when things simply are not going your way. Gratitude is paying attention to things that are already going well. Still, you need to focus and pay attention to really see them! What more is believing in things that are not real yet? So, yes, staying positive and trusting the Law of Attraction process can be hard at times.

However, do not forget that the Law of Attraction is all about how you feel—truly feel—inside. So, not feeling good or being doubtful can really get in the way of making it work for you. Imagine the Law of Attraction like a mirror—it only shows back the energy you put out there.

So, what can you do during tough days?

- **Shift your vibe.** Set aside any negative thoughts and focus on activities that can help you feel more positive and energized. How about putting in some extra time on your vision board? You could also whip up a fresh list of positive affirmations, curate a "feel good" playlist on Spotify, or even kick off a Law of Attraction journal. Those are all great ideas!

- **Remind yourself of all the great things that went your way before.** If you ever want proof of the power of the Law of Attraction, just think about all the good things you once hoped for that came true. Maybe you wanted to get a good score on an exam, get better at a hobby, or make a new friend, and it happened!

These moments show you that positive thinking works—and you were not even aware of the Law of Attraction then! Just imagine how much more great things can happen because you are more focused now. So, when you are feeling down, remind yourself of those wins to keep believing that more good things are on their way.

- **Keep your positive vibe high.** Avoid tough days by ensuring your positive energy is always "On." Imagine positivity like a campfire. For it to go on and on, you need to keep feeding it fresh wood, right? That is the same for the Law of Attraction—you have to keep feeding it with activities that bring you joy and do not stress you out.

If your illness is stopping you from doing your favorite things, then consider it the perfect opportunity to discover new activities that can lift your spirits. For example, if an injury is preventing you from going outdoors, think about new hobbies you can do indoors, like reading, trying kid-friendly cooking and baking (just make sure an adult is around to help), brainstorm ideas for a children's story, or even document your healing journey. There are plenty of cool things to do while you recover!

- **Believe in yourself.** Real-life talk: It is possible that not everyone you know will believe in the Law of Attraction. And you know what? No worries. It is okay if not everyone is on board because you do not need everyone to believe for it to work. The most important thing is that you go on and believe in yourself because this is all about how *you* feel and what *you* focus on.

When my little Emma was sick with leukemia, not everyone was on board with my belief that she would pull through. And truly, it did not matter. In my head, all that mattered was that "I" believed it. ☺

So, stay focused on your goals and your positive mindset, even if others do not understand or get it. It is your journey, and what matters most is that you believe in it!

Activity #14: Healing Focus Wheel

This exercise guides you to stay focused on getting better, even when you are not feeling your best.

Step 1. Write Down Your Current Feeling

In the center of the Focus Wheel below, write down how you are currently feeling about your illness or injury. It could be something like, "I am feeling weak," or "I am worried about how long it will take to heal." This is the starting point, and you are going to work on shifting those feelings, okay?

Step 2. Add Positive Healing Thoughts

In each of the outer sections, write a small, positive thought that feels true to you. Start with something that feels a bit more positive than your current feelings, like, "I know my body is trying hard to heal," or "Each day, I get a little stronger." Here is an example:

Your turn:

Step 3. Focus on Each Positive Thought

After filling in all the sections, take a few minutes to focus on each positive statement. Read each one out loud and believe in the healing message it offers. For example, if you wrote down, "I know my body is trying hard to heal," say it out loud and notice how this positive statement helps you feel better.

Part 4: Gratitude in Action for Healing

CHAPTER 15:
GRATITUDE IN NATURE

Nature has this amazing ability to help us heal. That is why you always hear people say, "Go outside and move" or "Go out and get some fresh air" whenever you are feeling down, sick, or stressed. What is up with that advice?

First off, getting some **fresh air** really helps clear your head and brings in more oxygen, which can totally boost your energy and help you focus better. Being outdoors, even for just a while, can boost your mood, reduce your anxiety, and help your body heal.

Then, we have the **sun** and all the incredible ways it can help us feel better. Sunlight is super important because it helps our bodies make **vitamin D**. This vitamin is key for strong bones and a healthy immune system, which means you can better fight off sickness. Being out in the sun can also boost your **serotonin** levels, which is that feel-good chemical in your brain, and it also helps with **melatonin**, the stuff that helps you sleep better.

Additionally, getting sunlight on you (in moderation and with sun protection) can also make you feel more energized! That is why you feel more active in the summer. But it is not all about buzzing energy; the sun can be calming too. Its warmth can help relax muscles and reduce pain.

And, of course, being in **nature** itself can be very healing. Nature attracts feelings of peace and joy because it helps your brain relax and disconnect from stress. Also, the outdoors has this amazing vibe, right? You have got leaves rustling, birds chirping, and that fresh smell of flowers and trees. It really helps chill you out, both in your mind and body.

So, if you really think about it, it is amazing how nature is literally JUST THERE to help you feel good and stay healthy.

Being in nature can also feel very magical. For example, the next time you are outdoors, take a step back and simply observe all the magical things that are happening in harmony around you.

You might notice butterflies gently landing on flowers. Is it not amazing how small, light, and dainty these creatures are? You do not hear them, but what a treat they are for the eyes to see!

You might notice birds singing in the trees. How can they be "up there," and yet you can still hear their voices so sharp and clearly?

And what about that awesome breeze flowing through the trees and rustling the leaves? Do you notice how they softly brush against your skin?

All of these little moments are happening in perfect harmony, like nature's way of showing how everything is connected. It is calming and peaceful, and it helps remind you of the beauty that is always around, even in the smallest details. Now, is that not something to be grateful for and feel positive about?

If you can take outdoor walks, that would be great! See the activity at the end of this chapter for a fun way to do that. But if that is not always possible, or your illness or injury is preventing you from doing that right now, then here are some amazing ideas for you!

1. **Sit by a window.** If you cannot head outside, chilling by a window is a great way to catch nature in action—like birds zooming by, trees dancing in the breeze, or clouds drifting overhead. These small observations help calm your mind and ease your stress, showing you that nature is always around to boost your mood.

2. **Open a window.** Even if you cannot be outdoors, opening a window lets in fresh air and the soothing sounds of nature, like birds chirping or leaves rustling. Getting some fresh air can really help you think better, and listening to nature sounds can totally make you feel more in tune with everything around you.

3. **Create a mini garden!** Growing small plants or flowers indoors is a great way to bring a bit of nature to your space. Watching a plant grow reminds you of the cycle of life and healing, giving you something positive to focus on while you recover.

   You can also decorate your space with natural items like rocks or seashells. These natural elements create a calming atmosphere, helping you feel connected to nature even while staying indoors.

4. **Watch nature videos.** If you cannot be outdoors, watching videos of beautiful landscapes or animals in their natural habitats is the next best

thing. This visual connection to nature helps ease stress and boosts feelings of calm and joy.

5. **Use nature sounds.** Play recordings of gentle rain, waves crashing, or forest sounds to create a peaceful space. These sounds help your mind relax, making you feel like you are immersed in nature's soothing presence.

6. **Manifest your favorite outdoor places.** Take a moment to close your eyes and picture a spot in nature that you love; maybe it is the beach or a peaceful forest. Visualizing yourself in these places can make you feel peaceful and reduce any stress or discomfort you are feeling.

7. **Look at nature photos.** Browse through photos of serene natural settings like mountains, lakes, or fields of flowers. Looking at these images can lift your spirits and give you a sense of calm, even if you are unable to physically be there.

8. **Meditate while imagining nature.** Close your eyes and picture yourself surrounded by nature. Whether it is a calm forest, a sunny beach, or a quiet meadow, this mental escape can help you feel relaxed and centered, promoting healing both in body and mind.

9. **Sit outside.** You do not need to go very far. If you have a little garden or balcony at home, just take a quick step outside for a few minutes. Find a comfy spot, whether that is sitting on a chair or on the ground, and enjoy the fresh air around you. Just taking a few minutes to listen to the birds, feel the breeze, or watch the clouds can really help you feel more in tune with nature and chill out a bit.

Activity #15: Mindful Outdoor Walks

This activity is a great way to connect with nature, feel gratitude, and stay positive about your healing journey.

Step 1. Safety First

Bring someone along! It can be fun to bring a friend, sibling, or family member on your walk. If this is not possible or if you prefer to walk alone, you should still always tell a parent or guardian where you are going and when you will be back. Just keep them in the loop!

Step 2. Prepare for Your Walk

Choose a calm outdoor space, like a park or garden near your home. (If you are going solo, always choose a place you know well.) And do not forget to wear comfy shoes and clothes! Alright, before you kick things off, take a deep breath and remember that this walk is all about noticing everything around you.

Step 3. Start Walking Slowly

Start off by taking your time and really noticing how your feet connect with the ground with each step you take. Next, check out how the ground feels under your feet. So, are you walking on soft grass, crunchy leaves, or smooth pavement right now? The aim is to really focus on what is happening right now. (This is called being **mindful**.)

Step 4. Use Your Senses

Next, you are going to use all your senses—but one at a time!— to really be aware of everything around you.

- **Look around**: Notice the colors, shapes, and movement of trees and plants around. What stands out to you?
- **Listen**: Focus on the sounds of birds, rustling leaves, or the wind. Can you hear something you have never noticed before?
- **Smell**: Take a deep breath. Is there a scent in the air, like flowers, rain, or fresh grass?
- **Feel**: Check out how the air feels on your skin. Is it warm, cool, breezy, or kind of ticklish?
- **Taste**: Stick your tongue out. Can you taste anything? You can also just take a deep breath and then swallow. Are you noticing any lingering taste in your mouth, like from toothpaste or some candy?

By the way, the goal is NOT to notice anything missing or out of sync. The aim here is simply to pay attention and take it all in. Once you start using all your senses like this, you'll be amazed at how many things you pick up on that you might have missed before!

Step 5. Be Grateful

As you walk, think about how nature is always growing and healing. Think about it—after a super intense storm, when trees are down and branches and leaves are everywhere, everything eventually goes back to normal, doesn't it? Imagine yourself going through the same thing—your body and mind are working hard to bounce back and help you feel better.

So, with each step you take, try to think of something you are grateful for in nature—like the fresh air, the sunshine, or the beauty you see around you.

Next, find a quiet spot to stop for a moment. Close your eyes and place your hand on your heart. Take three deep breaths, and with each breath, silently say, "Thank you for my healing." Imagine your body becoming stronger and healthier.

Step 6. Wrap It Up with Gratitude and Positivity

Before you finish your walk, say "Thank You" to nature for helping you feel calm and strong. Smile, knowing you are connected to the world around you and that everything is working together to help you bounce back.

CHAPTER 16: CREATIVE GRATITUDE

Like what we talked about in Chapter 3, gratitude becomes more powerful if you can find ways to show it. When you actively express your gratefulness, its power is magnified because you are turning your feelings (something internal) into actions (something visible or tangible).

When you want to thank someone, you might think about sending a quick Thank You note or even writing a Gratitude Letter. And these are both cool ideas! But there are plenty of other ways you can express your gratitude, like through art, writing, or even food! Yep, you can get all creative about it.

Why Creative Gratitude Matters

For You: Expressing gratitude in unique ways is very healing. When you focus on the good things in your life through drawing, writing, or making music, it helps you feel the positive vibes of gratitude for a longer time. It is like extending your "feel good" feelings, which is definitely great for your body!

For example, say "Aunt Sarah" dropped by and brought you some chicken soup on Saturday. When you take a moment to thank her, whether by drawing her a picture, writing a note, or even making up a little song about it, you are spending extra time to connect with that feeling of gratitude. This makes the positive, "feel-good" feelings from her kindness last looooonger, like pressing pause on a super happy moment.

Also, just the *process* of creatively expressing gratitude helps! Creativity releases positive energy through your body by engaging your mind and emotions in a way that makes you feel good, calm, and focused. Check out how creativity works:

- **You get "in the zone."** When you focus on a creative activity you like, you usually get into a state called "flow" or "in the zone." In this state, your mind feels happy and sharp, and you do not notice time flying by. And then, when you are done with what you are creating, you get a mighty boost of confidence because you know you created something meaningful.

- **You find cool ways to express your feelings.** Creativity allows you to share your thankfulness in ways that might be tricky to put into words. For example, if you are grateful for a friend who cheered you up when you felt really down, you might find a short message "not enough" and a gratitude letter "too much." In this case, maybe a handmade card with a picture of you two is the best way.

- **You activate that awesome mind-body connection again.** Creativity engages both your mind and body, especially with activities like dancing, crafting, or playing music. When your body is involved in the creative process, it activates positive energy in your physical movements.

For Others: Everyone likes to feel appreciated! And when people realize that you notice and appreciate what they do for you, there is a BIG chance they will keep showing you support and kindness.

Alright, let us dive into some cool and creative ways you can show your appreciation!

Gratitude Through Art

Art is like a window into your heart. When you create something, you are expressing yourself without needing to say a single word. To express thanks through art, you just need some basic stuff like paper, pencils, or paint. Just go for it and make whatever comes to your mind right now.

Think of something or someone you feel grateful for—maybe it is a person who has helped you or a beautiful part of nature, like a tree or the sun. Now, think about how you could express that vibe in a drawing or painting. Hey, remember that your art does not need to be flawless. What matters most is the process of making it happen.

When you draw or paint something that makes you feel thankful, you are giving yourself time to FOCUS on that feeling. And the more you focus on gratitude, the more you can see the good things around you!

Gratitude Through Crafts

Here is a super cool idea: Why not make something with your own hands to express your gratitude? You can create a friendship bracelet, knit something, or create a painted rock with a positive message. For your parents or caregiver, how does a "Thank You Coupon Book" sound?

You can create coupons for small acts of kindness or help, like "One Free Hug," "Breakfast Helper," "Laundry Folder for a Day," or "Dish Washing Assistant." You can decorate each coupon with markers, stickers, or drawings to make it extra special. Wouldn't that be awesome?!

Gratitude Through Photography

If you like snapping photos, you can totally use photography to catch those moments or things that you appreciate. It might be an amazing sunset, your awesome pet, or a super fun time hanging out with a sibling or friend. For example, you can put together a gratitude photo album or collage to remind yourself of these special moments.

Gratitude Through Baking or Cooking

If you enjoy cooking or baking, why not whip up a meal or a treat for someone to show your appreciation? Sharing food is a cool way to show you care about someone's help or kindness. Just be sure to have an adult help you in the kitchen—baking together can make the experience fun AND safe. Plus, cooking with someone lets you both share in the joy of creating something special.

Gratitude Through Writing

Writing is a powerful way to express gratitude. Sometimes, it is easier to write down what you feel inside than to say it out loud. If you want to thank someone, a Thank You note or gratitude letter is an awesome idea. If you want to start taking note of all the little and big things for which you are grateful, then maybe now is a great time to start a gratitude journal. (Do you find this a cool idea? If so, see **Chapter 17: Starting a Gratitude Journal** for more details.)

You can jot down something you are thankful for every day. It could be as simple as, "I am grateful for the sunny weather because I was able to sit outside," or "I am thankful for my friend who made me laugh so hard today. For a while, I forgot I was sick." When you write these things down, you are not just listing them—you are making them real and reminding yourself of the good in your life.

Writing also helps you remember good times, big or small. When you are having one of those off days, flipping through your gratitude journal can really remind you of all the awesome stuff you have going for you.

Gratitude Through Music

Music can totally shift your mood in a heartbeat! Listening to music that makes you feel happy or calm can totally help you remember all the things for which you should be grateful. But what if you took it a step further and created your own music to express gratitude?

Do not worry! You do not have to be a pro to create your own music. You can change the lyrics to a favorite song, or if you play an instrument, like the piano or guitar, you can create a short song about something or someone you are thankful for.

Activity #16: Creative Gratitude for Someone Special

Hey! How about we come up with a cool way to show your parent or main caregiver just how much you appreciate everything they do for you? Let us make it fun and creative!

Step 1. Think of Three Things You Appreciate

Think about three things your parent or caregiver does that really make you feel loved, safe, or happy. It can be stuff like whipping up your favorite meals, reading to you at bedtime, or just being around to listen whenever you need someone.

Step 2. Pick Your Creative Way to Say "Thank You"

Choose one of these ideas, or think of your own cool way to express gratitude!

- **Create a Drawing or Painting.** Make a piece of art that highlights something they do that you really value. It could be a sketch of you both whipping up something in the kitchen or just hanging out and having fun together. Add a small note that says, "Thank you _____, for all you do!"

- **Create a "Thank You" Poem or Letter.** Take a moment to write a short poem or letter expressing your gratitude and appreciation. You might want to kick things off with, "Hey [Mom/Dad/Caregiver], I just wanted to say thanks for..." and then go ahead and mention all the stuff you appreciate.

    Make sure to include some unique touches that really stand out. (If you need help writing your letter, see **Activity #7: Gratitude Letter**.)

- **Create a Gratitude Jar for Them.** Grab a jar and fill it up with little notes, each one sharing something you really love or appreciate about them. Can you imagine how they would feel each day reading a gratitude note from you?!

Step 3. Tada! Present Your Gift!

Once you are done with your awesome creative gratitude idea, present it to your parent or caregiver. You can give it to them directly or leave it somewhere as a surprise.

CHAPTER 17:
STARTING A GRATITUDE JOURNAL

A **gratitude journal** is like a cool notebook where you jot down all the stuff for which you are thankful. It might be something huge, like your family, or something simple, like your favorite sandwich. (Not kidding! An amazing sandwich is something to be grateful for, no?) Anyway, a gratitude journal is all about highlighting the good stuff in your life and really appreciating it. When you jot down these thoughts, you are really just giving yourself a little nudge to notice all the awesome stuff going on around you.

How Can Writing About Gratitude Attract More Reasons to Be Thankful?

When you zero in on what you are grateful for, your mind begins to pick up on even more things to appreciate. It is kind of like when you pick up a new word, and then all of a sudden, you start hearing it everywhere you go!

Also, remember our discussion on neuroplasticity. Keeping a gratitude journal rewires or trains your mind to sort of automatically look for the good in every day, even on tough days. Over time, you will start to see positive things all around you, and you will feel happier and more hopeful.

Further, as I said before, it is usually the little stuff (small moments) that creates the BIG, awesome ones. The problem is... well, we do not always remember the little moments, right? We do not intend to forget them; they just sort of sometimes slip our minds. But if you keep a gratitude journal where you take note of these things, then you will always have notes to look back on!

Top 10 Tips to Starting a Gratitude Journal

Do not know where to start? No worries; I got you. Here are some awesome tips to kick off your gratitude journal! Remember, being consistent and paying attention to the little things really makes a difference.

Step 1. Find a Notebook That Makes You Want to Write In It

What is your personal style when it comes to notebooks? Simple or fancy? Lots of space for writing, or lots of space to glue stuff on? Choosing the right journal is key because it should be something that makes you happy or inspires you every time you open it up.

Step 2. Make It a Habit

For the biggest chance that you will stay consistent with your journaling, pick a *specific time* each day to jot down your thoughts in your journal. It could be after school sessions or just before you sleep. Pick a time that is convenient for you. This way, you look forward to journaling and do not see it as a chore.

Now, everyone is different. Some people love to journal every day, while others prefer to write just once or twice a week. So here is my tip for you: try to journal at the same time every day to start and see how that feels. Give this schedule a go for about two solid weeks. If you find that daily writing is not for you, then write at the same time every Monday, Wednesday, and Friday (M-W-F). Still not working? How about every Tuesday and Thursday (T-Th)? Experiment with it and see what works.

Step 3. Thank You, Thank You, Thank You

In the book *The Magic* [8], author Rhonda Byrne suggests that we should say "Thank You" three times after sharing what we are grateful for. For example, "I am grateful for my awesome family. Thank you. Thank you. Thank you."

Repeating "Thank you" three times *deepens* your feelings of gratitude and reinforces its power! How? Do you remember our discussions about the **mind-body connection** in Chapter 2?

When you say "Thank You" often, it activates your brain's reward system, increasing the release of feel-good hormones like dopamine and serotonin even more. And the more "feel-good" chemicals you have in your body, the better because these neurotransmitters improve your mood, promote resilience, and reduce stress, allowing your body to recover more quickly.

To help you practice this powerful habit, let us look at more examples of expressing gratitude:

- **Supportive friends:** I am grateful for my best friend, Alex, who always tries to make me smile. Thank you. Thank you. Thank you.
- **A caring family:** I am grateful for my caring and supportive family. Thank you. Thank you. Thank you.
- **Access to technology and social media:** I am grateful for access to technology that lets me connect and learn while recovering. Thank you. Thank you. Thank you.
- **A favorite hobby or activity:** I am grateful for my favorite hobby, painting, because it brings me so much peace and joy. Thank you. Thank you. Thank you.
- **Gadgets:** I am grateful for my gadgets, like my laptop, which help me stay connected with friends, entertained when I am bored, and help me do my homework. Thank you. Thank you. Thank you.
- **A safe home environment:** I am grateful for having a safe place to live. Thank you. Thank you. Thank you.

- **School or educational opportunities:** I am grateful for my education and the chance to attend school. Thank you. Thank you. Thank you.
- **Encouraging mentors or teachers:** I am grateful for Mr. Kirkman. I think he is the most encouraging teacher I have right now. Thank you. Thank you. Thank you.
- **Healing:** I am grateful for my body's ability to heal and grow stronger every day. Thank you. Thank you. Thank you.

Step 4. Go Into the Details

A couple of years ago, there was a study by the University of California where students kept a gratitude journal for 10 weeks. Guess what they found? The more **details** students wrote about why they are grateful for something or someone, the higher the positive vibe they got from it![9] For example:

- I am grateful for Jessie because they took the time to come cover and help me with my homework today. Thank you. Thank you. Thank you.
- I am grateful because if Jessie did not come over, it would take me way longer to catch up with school stuff and finish my homework. Thank you. Thank you. Thank you.
- I am grateful Jessie came over because it made me less lonely today. Thank you. Thank you. Thank you.

Step 5. Share Your Feelings

When you jot down what you are grateful for, make sure to include how it makes you *feel* too. For example, "I am grateful for my Mom. I felt really *happy* when she let me keep my dog with me in bed. Thank you. Thank you. Thank you." Adding your feelings about what or whom you are grateful for shows how much that meant to you.

Step 6. Use "Prompts"

Do not know what to write in your journal? That is okay. Some days, you need to look just a little bit deeper to find stuff to be grateful for. These days, it helps to use "prompts," which are simple questions or ideas that can get you thinking. Here are some examples:

- What was something that made you happy today? Share something hilarious, or think of someone who brought a smile to your face today.

- Who is someone you really appreciate? Write about someone who gives you joy, comfort, support, or affection.

- What do you like most about yourself? What skill, quality, or something about you makes you feel good about yourself?

- What is something in nature you really like? One of my favorite parts of the outdoors has to be really tall trees! I like to think of them as nature's skyscrapers.

    When I am walking outdoors and see a big, majestic tree, I start to imagine how old they are and how much they have "seen" or experienced. Just imagine, they are out there, all day, every day, for years... and they just keep on growing! So, anyway, I start to feel in awe of these trees the more I look at them, and the next thing I do is touch the tree and say "Thank You" before I walk away.

- What do you enjoy most about school? At first, you may say... nothing! Hahaha! But really, give this one a think. Maybe school is where you meet up with your best friend, or maybe there is a class you secretly really enjoy, or maybe you have a teacher who is really kind and supportive of you.

- What is a meal or snack you really enjoy? Write about a food you really like and what makes it special for you.

- What is a cool memory you have? Share a day or moment that meant a lot to you.

- What do you really appreciate about your family or friends? Think about something you really admire in someone you care about. What makes them special to you?

- What is something cool you learned recently? Think about something interesting, like a fact, a skill, or a story.

- What is something you are excited to do soon? Describe something you're looking forward to that makes you feel happy and grateful.

Step 7. Include Unexpected or Unplanned Stuff

You know, sometimes unexpected things, like a problem or a challenge or just something you think you do not want, can turn out to be something you are grateful for.

For example, when my little Emma was sick and we would get an unexpected visitor, I used to get a bit annoyed. I was tired, Emma was tired, the house was a mess, etc. But you know what? Those unexpected visits cheered me up and cheered Emma up, and no one ever visited to look at our house. They visited because they cared and wanted to give their support. Today, I look at all those unplanned visits with much gratitude in my heart.

Step 8. Think "Simple"

Take a quick look around you. See anything you like or something that makes you smile? Maybe the pen you are holding reminds you of the strength in your hands, or a cozy blanket nearby makes you feel safe and warm. Sometimes, the simplest things can bring the most gratitude!

Step 9. Get Creative

If you are in the mood, throw in some cool drawings or doodles in your gratitude journal. If you cannot find the words, just sketch out the stuff you appreciate.

Step 10. Check Out Your Old Entries

Every now and then, take a moment to go through your past journal entries. You know, you do not have to always come up with something "new" to be grateful for. Often, just flipping through what you previously wrote and thinking about all the awesome stuff that has happened in your life can already make you feel even more thankful!

Advice for Common Journaling Problems

- **I cannot think of anything to be grateful for!** Hey, seriously, do not overthink this. Even on bad days, there is ALWAYS something to be grateful for. It could be something simple like, "I am grateful for a comfortable bed. Thank you. Thank you. Thank you." Or "I am grateful my parents can buy the medicine I need. Thank you. Thank you. Thank you." (**Tip**: Check out the "prompts" listed above for more journaling inspo!)

- **I do not feel happy even when I write in my journal.** ☹ Gratitude does not always mean instant happiness. But with constant practice, it can really help you shift your mood. Just keep going, and over time, you WILL notice small changes in how you see things.

- **I forget to write every day.** Keep your journal in a handy place where you will see it, like next to your bed. You can also set a reminder on your phone or ask someone to remind you.

- **It feels like I am writing the same things over and over.** That is okay! Would you rather that what you are grateful for disappears from your life? Of course not! So, keep being grateful, but maybe, this time, you can try to focus on the details. So, instead of writing, "I am grateful for my mom. Thank you. Thank you. Thank you," write something really specific about what she did that day, like "I am grateful my mom made my favorite breakfast today! Thank you. Thank you. Thank you."

- **I really tried… but I find journaling boring. Sorry!** No sweat. This most likely means that *writing* is not your thing. In this case, go back and check out **Chapter 16** again and find other creative ways to feel and express gratitude.

Part 5: Living a Life Full of Gratitude and Positive Intentions

CHAPTER 18:
STAYING GRATEFUL EVERY DAY

Gratitude does not have to be a complicated thing. Honestly, it is super simple to practice every day; no "mega effort" is required. And the cool thing is that the more you practice being thankful, the better you feel!

By now, you have learned that being grateful simply means noticing the good things in your life and taking a moment to appreciate them. Whether it is saying "Thank You" to someone, writing down something positive, or even just smiling at a nice memory—there are tons of simple ways to feel grateful every day.

To help you, here is a cool list of ideas for bringing a little bit of gratitude into each day, each week, or whenever you feel like it!

Gratitude Activities You Can Do Every Day

- **Kick off your morning with gratitude.** Before you get out of bed, take a deep breath, do a slow stretch, and take a moment to think of one thing you are thankful for before starting your day.

- **Say Thank You to someone.** Make it a point to say thank you to someone every single day. It could be a friend, a teacher, a family member, or even a stranger who held the door for you or helped you get something.

- **Gratitude Alarm.** Use your phone or watch to set a reminder that prompts you to take a moment and think about something you appreciate.

- **Daily Gratitude Walk.** While you are walking to school, heading to a friend's place, or just strolling around your yard, take a moment to think about what you appreciate. It could be the sky, the trees, or even your favorite songs.

- **Wrap Up Your Day with a Positive Vibe.** Before you hit the pillow, think of one awesome thing that happened today. Even if it is a small thing, it is always good to end your day on a high note!

   Tip: This can be part of a **Gratitude Stone** practice (**Chapter 7, Activity #7**), or you can write about it your **Gratitude Journal (Chapter 17)**.

Gratitude Activities You Can Do Every Week

- **Gratitude Jar.** Write down one thing you are grateful for on a small piece of paper and put it in a Gratitude Jar. At the end of the week or when the jar is full, pick one out and read what you have written. (See also **Chapter 5**, **Keep a "Little Things" gratitude jar**.)

- **Weekly Gratitude Themes.** Each week, pick a theme like "friends," "family," or "nature," and write about things you are grateful for in that category.

- **Gratitude Sharing Practice.** Once a week, during a meal with family or friends, share something you are thankful for that day or week. **Tip**: After sharing, encourage everyone to do the same!

Gratitude Activities You Can Do Occasionally

- **Gratitude Photo Album.** Bring out the amateur photographer in you! Take pictures of people, scenes, and things that make you happy or thankful, and create a special gratitude photo album to look back on. You can snap, print, and glue your pics on a board or create a digital one.

- **Write a Gratitude Letter.** Write a letter to someone who has made a difference in your life. It might be for a buddy, someone in your family, or a teacher. You do not have to send it if you do not want to. The important thing is to put into words how you feel. (Needs tips to write your letter? Check out **Activity #6: Gratitude Letter**.)

- **Random Acts of Kindness.** This is my favorite: Surprise someone with a kind act, like sharing a treat or helping without being asked, to show your gratitude.

CHAPTER 19:
ATTRACTING GOOD THINGS EVERY DAY

You remember everything we talked about the Law of Attraction, right? It sounds cool and mysterious, but it really is just a simple idea—what you focus on and believe in is what you attract into your life. That is it!

When you think positively and believe in yourself, you are sending out a signal to the universe that invites even more positive experiences and happy moments!

Sadly, this is also true for negative and unhelpful stuff. If you focus too much on feeling sad or frustrated because you are sick or injured, it is like telling the world you want more of those tough situations. Nope, you do not want that.

So, channel all your energy into focusing on positive thoughts and feelings, okay? To help you, here are tips you can do to keep attracting the good stuff.

Positive Activities You Can Do Every Day

- **Start with a Positive Thought.** Each morning, after thinking of one thing for which you are grateful, think of something you want to happen that day, like meeting a friend or having more energy than the day before. This simple positive thought helps you start the day with good energy and focus!

- **Use "I Am" Statements.** Say something positive about yourself, like "I am kind" or "I am strong." This helps you believe in yourself and attract positive vibes all day long. (See also **Chapter 12: Affirmations**.)

- **Smile!** Did you know that smiling often can really boost your mood? I know it can be hard to keep smiling when you are sick or in pain, but just give it a shot. You might just be surprised at how a simple thing can totally switch up your day.

Tip: Not feeling it? Half-smile it!
Not in the mood for a full-on, teeth-baring grin? That is okay. Go for a half-smile like the famous Mona Lisa does.

Just relax your face and shoulders and let the sides of your mouth curve upwards a tiny bit. Now, you should *feel* this smile even if no one notices it. Just put on a calm facial expression. Like half-smile, but the rest of your face looks bored.

But why would you even want to do this? Well, remember our talks about the mind-body connection? Usually, what you feel inside, you tend to show outside. If you are sad, you frown; if you are angry, you clench your teeth or hands. So, why not turn things around? Even if you feel a bit down, half-smile your way to start feeling better and telling the universe to start sending positive stuff!

- **Positive Self-Talk.** NO ONE is perfect. If you make a mistake, please do not say, "I am bad at this," or "I suck!" Instead, try saying, "I am learning," or "I will get better at this soon." This positive self-talk builds confidence.

- **Gratitude Practice.** Gratitude is being thankful for what you already have. When you get into the habit of being thankful, you will attract more and more things to be thankful for! Cool, huh?

Positive Activities You Can Do Every Week

- **Visualize Your Goals.** Take a moment each week to close your eyes and think about something you really want to come true, like picking up a new hobby or meeting a new friend. Believe it, picture it happening, and feel the joy it brings. (**Tip**: Start making a **Vision Board**! See **Activity #14: Healing Vision Board** for tips on how to make one.)

It is VERY important to know what you want. As I mentioned before, the universe does not guess. It is actually more like a delivery van—it can only bring what you order!

- **Create a "Positive Energy" Object.** Pick a small item, like a pebble or a bracelet, and think of it as your good-luck charm. Hold it whenever you want a boost of positivity and focus.

- **Power Pose!** This is something similar to positive self-talk or affirmations, but instead of saying positive things about yourself, you are applying positive body language!

Remember, what you focus on is what you attract, and that can be through your words *and* your actions. Now, I understand that you might be sad, down, or even angry because you are unwell. But maybe these feelings are making you sit, stand, or even walk a certain way.

For example, you might frown, keep your shoulders slumped, or cross your arms tightly around you a lot without even realizing it. Now, these actions broadcast "signals" that you are unhappy. Now, you do not want to attract more unhappiness, right? So what you are going to do is change your body language to a more positive posture.

For starters, try standing tall with your shoulders back and giving a big smile. You can even put your hands on your hips like a superhero! This "power pose" sends a message to your brain that you are strong and positive, helping you attract more of that good energy.

- **Take Positive Breaks from Screens.** When you are sick, it is easy to spend a lot of time online. Watching videos, playing online, or chatting with friends can be fun, but too much screen time can overwhelm you too.

You might feel tired or even a bit sad if you are seeing things you cannot do right now. So, try taking some screen breaks to focus on activities that help you feel good in REAL LIFE, like reading, writing, drawing, or spending time with family.

Taking breaks from screens helps you focus on your own healing journey and lets you build positivity by doing things that lift you up!

Positive Activities You Can Do Occasionally

- **Set Monthly Intentions + Positive Actions.** At the start of each month, pick one area of your life to focus on, like "healing," "friendship," "family," or "learning." Write down the "ultimate goal" you want to attract in that one area, and then think about all the teeny tiny actions you can take every day to make it happen!

- **Challenge Yourself with Fresh Goals.** Every couple of months, think about setting a new goal or challenge, like diving into a new activity or picking up a new skill. New challenges present great opportunities for new positive experiences!

- **Be a Walking Ray of Sunshine!** If you want to attract positivity and happiness, YOU need to be a source of positivity and happiness. This is when the Law of Attraction is at its most powerful and effective!

This is NOT as hard as you think, you know. You can do random acts of kindness, little things that other people appreciate.

You can also choose to do BIG things if you like. For example, wake up one day and say to yourself, "Today is THE day that I will really help someone!" For instance, say that your sibling has been constantly nagging you to borrow something of yours. Why not today be the day you gift wrap it and give it to them like a present?

You can also do something for your parents or caregiver. For example, you can completely tidy up your room and maybe even do the laundry and fold your clothes. (Plus points if you fold *their* clothes too!)

CHAPTER 20:
THE LIGHT AT THE END OF THE TUNNEL

When you are dealing with something tough, like being sick or recovering from an injury, it is totally normal to feel frustrated or down. But there is one person who can really help you through this more than anyone else—YOU!

When you focus on taking care of yourself and building good habits, you will feel more empowered, and that is important because it is not your illness or injury that controls your life—it is you who is in charge. And when you feel in charge, your mind and body feel confident, and you are again building on that positive energy! So, let us look at a few ways you can help yourself stay calm, balanced, and confident.

Looking After Yourself

Healthy Eating and Sleeping Habits

You already know that your body is like a battery, and eating well and getting enough sleep are two big ways to keep it power-charged! Eating healthy foods gives your body the energy it needs to bounce back and feel powerful. Getting a solid night's sleep is also super important. It helps your body chill out, recover, and feel way better the next day.

Here are some cool tips for eating and sleeping better:

- **Pick Foods That Power You Up!** When you are sick, you might always want to reach out for comfort food or feel-better food like mac n' cheese or cookies. Indulging in these is okay every now and then, but it is best if you go for foods and drinks that help your body heal. So, as much as possible, avoid fried food, processed foods, and too much sweets.

- **Keep Drinking Water.** Make sure you are sipping on water all day to help your body stay in top shape. Staying hydrated is super important for your body to recover and feel better.

- **Stick to a Sleep Schedule.** You know, being sick does not mean getting a license to sleep and wake up anytime you want. (Sorry!) Your body thrives on routine, so try to go to bed and wake up at the same time every day.

Handling School Stuff

Schoolwork might feel extra hard or frustrating when you are trying to deal with illness. But staying on top of things, even just a little, can really give you that feeling of achievement and help you stay in the loop with your friends and classmates. Here are some tips to help you manage schoolwork:

- **Take It One step at a Time.** If school feels like a lot, break it down into smaller pieces you can handle. Try to concentrate on one thing, task, or topic at a time.

- **Ask for Help.** If you are struggling, just talk to a teacher, a friend, or a family member. They are there for you! They can totally break things down for you or share some cool tips to make it all a bit easier. Also, do not be scared to ask for some leeway. For example, if you are feeling tired or need extra time to finish an assignment, let your teacher know—they may be able to give you more time or adjust things so you do not feel overwhelmed.

- **Focus on Progress.** Acknowledge those little victories, like completing a page of homework or grasping a new concept. Every little step matters, even if it seems like it is taking forever.

- **Take Study Breaks.** It is important not to overwhelm yourself by doing everything all at once. Make sure to take some quick breaks to refresh yourself, then dive back into your studies with a clear head.

Dealing with Mood Swings

Emotional roller-coaster much? That is okay. It is totally normal to feel super happy and hopeful one moment and then a bit frustrated or even scared the next. That is just how it goes sometimes, especially when you are dealing with stress and healing. To help you deal with mood swings better, here are some tips:

- **Just… Breathe.** If you are feeling really intense emotions, just stop for a second and take some slow, deep breaths. This really helps chill you out, both in your head and your body.

- **Express Your Feelings.** Sometimes, putting your feelings down on paper or sketching them out can really help you let them go. You can also chat with someone you really trust about what you are dealing with.

- **Make a "Feel-Better" Routine.** Prepare a go-to list of things to do when you are feeling low, like diving into a favorite book, listening to some music, or hanging out with your pet. It is important to make this list NOW, not when you are in the middle of feeling sad.

- **Remember: Feelings Do Not Last Forever.** Did you know that not a single emotion lasts forever? It is just part of being human to feel different emotions throughout the day. Some research even says people can go through more than 30 different feelings every day depending on A LOT of things like what they might have seen or heard, their physical health, their surroundings, and a bunch of other stuff.[10]

So, when you are on the "down side" of that emotional roller coaster, remind yourself that it is okay because it is temporary. Using phrases like "I'm trying my hardest" or "This feeling will not stick around forever" can really make a difference.

Staying Connected with Family and Friends

Sometimes, you might want to pull away from people, even those you love. One reason for this might be that it is just really hard to "deal" with your illness or injury right now, so you do not want to spend any energy on others. It might also be that it is just too sad or painful to see everyone else being "healthy and fit," so you want to avoid them. Other times, well, maybe it is just hard to accept help, and you would rather do things on your own so people do not see you as "weak" and pity you.

But you know what? By avoiding connection, you might be missing out on feeling supported and actually starting to feel better! So, let us try shifting how you see this "staying connected" thing, shall we?

- **Instead of feeling sorry for yourself because you need help, think of it as an opportunity to LET others show you love and care.** Your friends and family are there because they want to support you.

Accepting their help can make them feel good, too, because they are helping you feel stronger.

- **Instead of pretending to be upbeat when others are around, just be yourself.** Let people know how you are really feeling, whether it is hopeful, tired, frustrated, or anything in between. It takes a lot of strength to be honest, and it helps bring you closer to the people who care about you.

- **Instead of ghosting friends, let them know HOW they can best support you.** Tell them when you need a laugh, a chat, or maybe even just a listening ear. Real friends will appreciate knowing how to be there for you in a way that makes YOU feel comfortable.

Handling Conflicts with Siblings or Friends

Sometimes, when you are sick, you are not in the best of moods, and it is easy for small things to turn into big arguments. Sadly, arguing with your siblings or friends can totally bring you down even more, so figuring out how to keep things chill is super important. Here are some suggestions for dealing with disagreements:

- **Hit "Pause."** If you start to feel angry, try taking a deep breath or counting to ten before you say anything. This can help you stay cool and think things through instead of just getting mad.

- **Share Your Feelings Using "I" Statements.** Have you ever noticed that when people are angry or annoyed at someone, they tend to start their sentences with the word "You?" For example, "You are always at my back." or "You never listen to me!" or "You keep bothering me!"

Statements like this can make the other person feel like you are blaming them, which can lead to hurt feelings and bigger arguments.

So, if someone has upset you, try using "I feel" statements to express what YOU feel or think. For example:

Not: You are always at my back!
But: I feel overwhelmed when I have too many reminders about resting or taking my medicine.

Not: You never listen to me!
But: I feel ignored when I try to explain how I am feeling and feel misunderstood.

Not: You keep bothering me!
But: I feel frustrated when I do not get time to relax on my own, even for just a little while.

- **Look for the Middle Ground.** Finding a compromise can make things easier for everyone involved. For example, instead of focusing on what you want versus what others want, how about thinking about it this way: Hmmm, I wonder what can **we** do so that we both feel good about this?

- **Take a Breather.** If things get a bit too heated, it is totally fine to step away for a bit and talk again when you and the other person are feeling calmer. This can help stop little problems from blowing up into huge arguments. But do not just walk away, okay? You can say something like, "I need a moment to calm down so we can talk better," or "I want to make sure I say this the right way, so I need a little time please." This way, you are being respectful and giving both of you a chance to cool off.

Dealing with Setbacks

Sometimes, things do not go as we plan them. For example, suppose you thought you would be fully recovered by a certain date and started planning to go to a friend's birthday party, only to be told that you are not quite ready yet. Or maybe you thought you would be able to play your favorite sport again but realize your body still needs more time to heal. These moments, when things feel unfair or disappointing, are called **setbacks**.

Setbacks are like little bumps in the road that delay your arrival at your destination. Now, some people may get totally bummed out, sad, or angry when setbacks happen, but like what we discussed with the Law of Attraction, you should definitely try to shift your thoughts and emotions to a more positive frequency. Otherwise, you might accidentally attract more setbacks. Yikes!

Also, setbacks do not always have to be a bad thing, you know. Sure, you may feel sad that you still cannot do what you want to do. But then again, if you do something before your body is truly ready, *full recovery* may take even longer. You do not want that, do you? You want to be 100% A-Okay before you take on things again.

Now, let us check out some easy ways to turn setbacks into opportunities to feel better, stay positive, and keep pushing ahead!

- **Remember: Feel them, and release them.** It is totally okay to feel sad, frustrated, or even angry when things do not turn out how you hoped. It is totally okay to let your feelings out—if you need to cry, go for it or chat with someone about what is on your mind. Hey, just know that your feelings really matter, and sharing them can help you feel a little lighter.

Tip: Why not grab a notebook or journal and jot down what you are feeling? It can really help! If you do not want to write, just draw or doodle what you are feeling! Sometimes, just seeing your feelings on paper makes them easier to handle. Also, if you want, try the **Balloon Release** activity in Chapter 8.

- **Look for the Bright Side.** Finding the bright side means searching for the positives that are tucked away during challenging moments. For example, being "forced" to stay home might be a chance for you to dive into a new book or hobby. By the way, this is not about pretending everything is awesome all the time; it is more about being a detective and spotting those little bits of good that can come out of a setback or the unexpected.

Tip: Whenever you are feeling down, see if you can spot just one little thing to appreciate right then and there. It could be having time to have a long bubble bath or having extra time to play with your pet.

- **Come Up With a Positive Mantra.** A **mantra** is a short, positive saying or statement you can say to yourself during difficult times. It helps you feel more in charge and prepared to push through, even when things get rough. For setbacks, you can have a mantra like, "Well, this moment is hard, but I have got this!" or "I do not like this, but it is okay. Tomorrow will be better."

Tip: Choose a mantra that makes you feel calm or brave. Say it to yourself whenever you are feeling upset or worried.

- **Concentrate on What You Can Do.** During setbacks, it is super easy to focus on what you **cannot** do right now. But shifting your focus to what you **can** do can help you feel more positive! Also, setbacks usually prevent you from doing ONE thing, but there are at least a dozen other cool things you can do, so it is good to remember that.

Tip: Make a **Can-Do** list! Grab a pen and paper or your notebook and start listing things you can enjoy doing, even while you are healing.

- **Patience, Patience, Patience.** Healing takes time, and even though it kinda feels like things are going way too slow—things are improving! Remember, your body is a 24-hour superhero that is doing its best to help you recover. So, be kind and patient with your body. Just like a plant takes time to grow, your body also needs time to get back to feeling strong. Believing that you are moving forward, even in tiny steps, can really help you stay positive.

Tip: Every night, write down one tiny sign that you are making progress, like "I had more energy today" or "I felt a bit better after taking a break." These little victories prove that you are moving ahead. (If you do not want to write, try the **Gratitude Stone** activity in Chapter 7.)

- **Surround Yourself with Good Vibes.** It would be great if you could surround yourself with things that bring you joy and boost your mood. You might want to put up some cool drawings, check out those happy photos, listen to your favorite tunes, watch feel-good movies, or watch some hilarious videos. Being surrounded by positivity makes it easier to feel good, even on challenging days.

Tip: Create a **positivity corner** in your room! This can be a special space where you place or hang your vision board. You can also place your favorite cozy items here, like a soft blanket, a favorite book, or a poster with a positive mantra. You might also want to add little notes that make you smile and inspire you every day.

Everyone faces setbacks—it is just part of life. Even the toughest people out there have times when things just do not work out the way they hoped. The important thing is to take setbacks on the chin and bounce back better! It might feel tough right now, but trust me, as time goes on, you will realize that every setback has helped you become braver and stronger.

CHAPTER 21:
SHARING YOUR STORY

When you practice gratitude, it is like building up a special kind of energy that helps you feel happier, stronger, and more positive, right? Well, there is this thing called **gratitude momentum**. Think of it like a snowball rolling down a hill—it starts small but gets bigger and bigger. This means that the more you focus on being grateful and expressing thankfulness, the stronger and more intense the positive energy you generate.

Now, one of the coolest ways to keep your gratitude momentum going is by sharing your gratitude journey with others. And here's the cool part, according to the Law of Attraction, if you THINK positive thoughts and DO positive things, you attract even more good things into your life. Wowza!

Sharing your story and inspiring others is kind of like the gift that keeps on giving. You see, when you open up about your journey, you are not just helping yourself—you are giving others hope and support, too. Here are a few ways you can do this:

- **Reach out to someone who you know is also ill.** Sometimes, knowing that someone else understands what you are going through makes reaching out to them a little easier. So, how about sending a message or writing a card to let them know that they are not alone? And if they want, they can totally get back to you if they want to know what is keeping your spirits up. Your story and encouragement might be exactly what they need, you know?

- **Check out online and offline groups or communities.** If you want to connect with kids dealing with similar health issues or injuries, that is a great idea too. You can ask your parents, caregiver, or even your doctor if they know any groups you can join. You can also check out some online groups where kids like you share their experiences, struggles, and good times. Just make sure to chat with a parent or caregiver before jumping into any online group, okay? You want to be sure you are joining a safe space.

- **No need to overshare; just start with small stories.** Once you have connected with someone or a group, start with sharing something simple or small. For example, you can mention that getting support from family and friends encouraged you to try to support other kids, or you can share that keeping a gratitude jar or writing in a gratitude journal helps you stay positive. When you share these stories, it is like bringing back those awesome times and attracting even more good experiences like them.

- **Start your own "Gratitude Group."** How about asking a few friends if they would like to share one thing they are grateful for each week? It could be a fun way to connect and appreciate the good stuff in life together!

- **Be a gratitude role model.** When others see you practicing gratitude regularly, they will pick up on the good vibes coming from you. And your example could totally inspire them to give it a shot as well.

According to the Law of Attraction, what you focus on and share often comes back to you, so keep on sharing and spreading gratefulness and positivity. Remember, your healing story has the power to generate and attract positive energy—one thankful moment at a time!

CHAPTER 22:
GRATITUDE AND POSITIVITY BEYOND INJURY AND ILLNESS

So far, you have been laser-focused on how you can use **gratitude** and **positivity** to help you heal. But did you know that these superpowers can also benefit you long after your recovery?

Think of gratitude and the Law of Attraction as your amazing go-to tools for experiencing an awesome life! You see, we all have some sort of "life magnet" inside us. So, by making gratitude and positivity part of who you are as a person, you will continue to feel more positive, notice good things more often, and pretty much just keep on attracting good stuff! And who does not want that, right? So, check out these tips to make these practices a lasting part of your life!

- **Always start each morning with a positive intention.** Here is something to think about: people do not wake up thinking, "I want to be unhappy today" or "Today will suck," but... most people do not think the opposite either. Kinda funny, no? So, just imagine how AWESOME things can be if you always **choose** to start your day with a happy and positive vibe.

    For example, when you wake up each morning, take a deep breath and say or think, "Today is a good day to have a great day!" You can also mention a goal like "Today, I am going to 100% focus on _____."

- **Maintain a gratitude practice.** As you may have noticed, this book has PLENTY of gratitude activities. Now, as you go through them, see which ones really connect with you or which ones you really like doing. Maybe you prefer to make Gratitude Mind Maps or write in a Gratitude Journal. If you prefer to keep things simple, maybe having a Gratitude Stone or filling Gratitude Jars is more your thing. The important thing is to pick a gratitude habit and make it part of who you are for years and years.

- **Keep on attracting the good stuff!** Take time to think about all the cool things you want in your life—whether it is learning something new, receiving an award at school, winning a sports competition, meeting a new friend, going on an awesome adventure, or even dreaming about your future job and buying the car of your dreams!

Regularly visualizing what you want in life and believing that you will receive them keeps the Law of Attraction process always in motion for you. For this reason, I strongly encourage you to keep on creating Vision Boards. (See also **Bonus: My "Wishes Come True" Box** at the end of this book!)

- **Be a master at turning setbacks into learning moments.** I am sorry to tell you, but life will always have ups and downs. However, gratitude and the Law of Attraction teach that HOW you respond to these setbacks matters. So, whenever things do not go as planned, ask yourself, "What can I learn from this?" Looking for lessons during tough times keeps you from feeling stuck and helps you stay positive.

- **Always believe in yourself and be your own cheerleader!** It is great to have the love, care, and support of people in our lives, but it is also important to be your own cheerleader.

  This means that even when things are difficult, do not be negative or too hard on yourself. Instead, always use kind and encouraging words when talking to yourself. For example, instead of thinking, "I suck! I am hopeless at this!" think, "I do not know this... *yet*," or "I am still learning. I will get better at this soon." Remember, positive self-talk helps attract positive experiences!

- **Be kind and spread good energy.** When you are kind to others, you are radiating good energy. The Law of Attraction sees this and will work on sending kindness and good vibes back to you.

- **Always reflect on progress.** When you are ill or injured, the focus should be on what you **can** do, not on what you cannot do, right? Well, in life, it is always better to focus on progress rather than setbacks, mistakes, missed opportunities or goals, or perfection. Thinking about how far you have come keeps you motivated on your goals and reminds you how gratitude and positivity have helped along the way.

  Also, do not wait for big achievements to feel proud. Celebrating small wins makes life more fun and positive!

- **Make time for activities that bring you joy and the people you love.** Doing stuff that brings you happiness is a big part of staying positive. Playing sports, making art, exploring the outdoors, or just hanging out and laughing with friends can really keep the good vibes going.

Also, make time for the important people in your life. You know, even though there may be times you do not feel it, **YOU are important to the people around you**. So, it really helps if you actively participate in these relationships.

For example, instead of waiting around for someone to come up with a cool idea for a bonding moment, why not take the lead and come up with something yourself? Like inviting a friend over, getting your family together for a game, or planning a cool outing.

When you step up, you are not just opening doors to more fun, but you are also letting everyone know that you really care about the time you spend together. You're going to create awesome memories and strengthen your bonds, which will totally make you and your friends and family feel happier and more connected.

Conclusion

Wow, what a wonderful thing you have done for your healing journey! It is my sincere hope that you have come to realize the amazing and powerful roles that **Gratitude** and the **Law of Attraction** can play in your recovery. So, how about a quick recap?

Gratitude is the practice of being grateful for everything that is going well instead of dwelling on what is not going right or what you wish to be different. The **Law of Attraction is the practice of focusing your energy and actions on what you want to happen** instead of worrying and struggling with what is going on right now.

Gratitude and the Law of Attraction are healing superpowers because they (1) help your mind focus on the positive, (2) stimulate your body to release feel-good chemicals that help with healing, and (3) they act like magnets that attract more good things into your life!

Yes, it can be a very trying time right now, but I truly want you to understand that YOU have the power to change your situation for the better. The "frequency" of your thoughts and feelings matters, and every grateful thought, every act of kindness, and every positive action adds up to make your healing experience more uplifting and powerful.

Also, remember that your body is a living, breathing energy battery and that gratitude and positivity attract the energy you need to recharge it. So, chin up! Healing takes time and patience, but with a grateful heart and a positive attitude, you are creating a brighter and healthier future for yourself.

Bonus: My "Wishes Come True" Box

This activity is a fun way to DREAM BIG and put your wishes in a safe and special place. It is a cool alternative to a Vision Board if you prefer to keep your wishes more private.

Each time you add a wish, think of it as sending a secret but powerful message to the universe about what you want to happen!

Step 1. Pick a Box
Grab a small shoebox or any box with a lid that you use to store your wishes. This will be your special "Wishes Come True" box, so make sure it is something you like and can have fun decorating.

Step 2. Jazz Up Your Box
Grab some stickers, markers, glitter, or whatever you think is cool to jazz up the outside of the box. Make it vibrant and one-of-a-kind! You can even add some stars, hearts, or drawings that make you happy.

Step 3. Gather Your Supplies
Grab some small pieces of paper or note cards and a pen, pencil, or marker. You can also use colored pencils or crayons to make your wishes stand out.

Step 4. Write Your Wish!
Take a quiet moment to think about what you want to happen. This could be recovering faster, making new friends, doing well on a test, getting a visit from

someone special, or anything you like. Hey, it is your box, so do not hold back!

Next, write each wish on its own piece of paper. Do not forget to decorate it or add a small drawing next to your wish to make it more visual.

Step 5. Put Your Wishes in the Box
Fold up your wish paper and pop it inside your box. Think of it as "sending" your wish out into the universe.

Step 6. Your Wish Is On Its Way to Being Granted!
This part is super important: for each wish paper you put in the box, believe that the universe received your wish and is putting things into play to make it come true. You do not know when your wish will come true, but trust that it will happen in its own time.

So, whenever you drop a wish paper in your magic box, completely let it go! Let yourself feel excited, knowing that your wish is out there, and enjoy the journey as you wait for it to happen.

Step 7. Keep Adding New Wishes
Whenever you think of a new wish or dream, just jot it down and put it into the box. Add as many as you want; there are no limits to what the universe can provide!

Step 8. Check Your Wishes
After a few weeks or months, open your box, read through your wishes, and see which ones have come true! Be sure to keep an open mind because

sometimes, your wishes come true in ways you totally did not see coming, which is part of the fun!

For example, maybe you wished for a new friend, and while you did not meet someone new right away, you ended up growing closer to a classmate you had not really talked to much before. Or maybe you wished to get better at a sport, and instead of just improving in one area, you discovered a whole new game you love playing. The universe loves surprises and sometimes sends unexpected answers to your wishes. Cool, right?

A Message from Emma

Hey there! I am Emma! 👋 I just wanted to tell you a bit about my own healing journey. Like my mom said, I was diagnosed with leukemia when I was 18 months old. Honestly, I do not remember much about that time! I guess it was because I was too young.

But ever since my mom decided to tell our story in this book, I have had so many questions! One of them was, "Mom, didn't you ever think I would not get better?" My mom, determined now as she was then, said, "No!"

"Oh, come on, Mom, you never had any doubts? Not even a little one?"
"No. I was always focused on positivity. I always believed you would be cured."
"What about Dad?
"Dad was very sad, of course. But then..."
"What?"
"My positivity influenced him. He did not have a choice but believe you will get better!"

I was in and out of the hospital for two years because I had to go through a lot of treatments, and for sure, my family had some really tough days. But my mom was the "sunshine," "gratitude force," and "positivity energy ball" we all needed! And then the miracle happened—the doctors said my leukemia was gone.

I still had to go for check-ups every six months for the next five years, but after that, we got the awesome news that I was officially cancer-free. I was 8 years old back then.

During those years, my mom never wavered and made sure I knew about the power of gratitude and staying positive so I could always have great health and attract everything my heart desires—even when things seemed hard.

Now, at 21, I embrace gratitude and positivity every single day. And because it is a natural part of me, I do not put in any "effort" to be grateful or positive, it just comes naturally.

I automatically look for—and find—the good in every day, even if it is something small. I find joy in a funny joke, a warm hug, or even just sitting and having time for myself. I really value the things and people in my life, and I make sure I express it.

Of course, there are always some "bad days," but even then, I believe that no matter what challenges I face, I can find strength in gratitude and attract good energy into my life. I am positively hopeful and giddy with excitement about what the future holds for me.

Thank you for reading this book and for opening your heart to gratitude and positivity. I really hope our story and these ideas help you on your journey toward healing and life-long happiness.

Beaming you gratitude and positivity,
Emma

References

1 Emmons, R. A., & McCullough, M. E. (2003). Counting blessings versus burdens: An experimental investigation of gratitude and subjective well-being in daily life. *Journal of Personality and Social Psychology, 84*(2), 377–389. https://doi.org/10.1037/0022-3514.84.2.377

2 Dunn, L. (2021, November 24). Gratitude is good for your health. TODAY.com. https://www.today.com/health/be-thankful-science-says-gratitude-good-your-health-t58256

3 Brown, J., & Wong, J. (2017, June 6). *How gratitude changes you and your brain*. Greater Good. https://greatergood.berkeley.edu/article/item/how_gratitude_changes_you_and_your_brain

4 Nicioli, T. (2024, July 12). *Practicing gratitude could help you live longer, new study says*. CNN. https://edition.cnn.com/2024/07/12/health/gratitude-benefits-longer-life-wellness/index.html

5 *The power of the placebo effect*. Harvard Health. (2024, July 22). https://www.health.harvard.edu/newsletter_article/the-power-of-the-placebo-effect. Reviewed by Howard E. LeWine, MD, Chief Medical Editor, Harvard Health Publishing; Editorial Advisory Board Member, Harvard Health Publishing

6 Sherman, D. K., Bunyan, D. P., Creswell, J. D., & Jaremka, L. M. (2009). Psychological vulnerability and stress: The effects of self-affirmation on sympathetic nervous system responses to naturalistic stressors. *Health Psychology, 28*(5), 554–562. https://doi.org/10.1037/a0014663

7 Koole, S. L., Smeets, K., van Knippenberg, A., & Dijksterhuis, A. (1999). The cessation of rumination through self-affirmation. *Journal of Personality and Social Psychology, 77*(1), 111–125. https://doi.org/10.1037/0022-3514.77.1.111

8 Byrne, R. (2012). *The Magic*. Atria Books.

9 Oppland, M. (2017, April 28). *13 most popular gratitude exercises & activities*. PositivePsychology.com. Retrieved March 21, 2022, from https://positivepsychology.com/gratitude-exercises/

10 Trampe, D., Quoidbach, J., & Taquet, M. (2015). Emotions in everyday life. *PLOS ONE*, *10*(12). https://doi.org/10.1371/journal.pone.0145450

www.ingramcontent.com/pod-product-compliance
Lightning Source LLC
Chambersburg PA
CBHW082246090526
44585CB00021BA/2460